THE ♕ CHESS
KID'S ♗ BOOK
of Checkmate

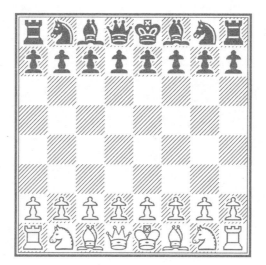

David MacEnulty
Foreword by Bruce Pandolfini

Random House
Puzzles & Games

The Chess Kid's Book of Checkmate

This book is available for special discounts for bulk purchases for sales promotions or premiums. Special editions, including personalized covers, excerpts of existing books, and corporate imprints, can be created in large quantities for special needs. For more information, write to Special Markets/ Premium Sales, 1745 Broadway, MD 6-2, New York, NY, 10019, or e-mail *specialmarkets@randomhouse.com*

Visit the Random House Reference Web site: www.randomwords.com

Typeset and printed in the United States of America.

Library of Congress Cataloging-in-Publication Data

American Bar Association family legal guide.—3rd ed.
p. cm.
Rev. ed. of: Family legal guide. Rev. ed. c1994.
Includes index.
ISBN 0-609-61042-2 (alk. paper)—ISBN 0-375-72077-4 (trade pbk. : alk. paper)
1. Law—United States—Popular works.   2. Law—United States—Miscellanea.
I. Title: Family legal guide.   II. American Bar Association.   III. Family legal guide.

KF387.Y655 2004
349.73—dc22
2004041855

ISBN: 0-8129-3594-2

1st Edition
0 9 8 7 6 5 4 3 2 1

*For teaching me the importance of breaking complex
ideas down into simple, easy-to-understand units,
this book is dedicated to*

Eric Whitney

Acknowledgments

My thanks to Mitchel Fitzko and Taghian M. Taghian for their thoughtful reading of the manuscript and their valuable suggestions for improvement. I am also very grateful to Bruce Pandolfini for his assistance with this book, for generously agreeing to write the forward, and for introducing me to the joys of teaching.

Contents

Part Four

Foreword
by Bruce Pandolfini

Prior to 1972 the Soviet Union was the chess storybook's Emerald City, and its minions dominated the art and science of teaching the universal game. But Brooklynite Bobby Fischer changed all that after he defeated the Russian world champion, Boris Spassky, in Reykjavik, Iceland in the greatest chess match ever played.

Before Fischer snatched the title chess lessons in the United States consisted largely of a play session between teacher and student, peppered, perhaps, with a commentary and analysis. Organized courses, curricula, and educational chess literature were rarities.

Fischer's triumph attracted millions of neophytes to the game, and they expected more thoroughgoing approaches to chess instruction. A number of strong players tried to fill the demand, but though many were adept at competition, few were conversant in the craft of teaching fundamentals. Some did succeed, however. Their groundbreaking work enabled the next group of chess coaches and trainers to develop a cogent pedagogy with intellectual clout. But it wasn't until the mid-1980s, with the rise of computers and support-based large-scale academic formats, that educators were able to devise more reliable chess regimens.

David MacEnulty was among the leaders in these seminal efforts. From the early 1990s David began to formulate the principles of chess instruction for actual use in school settings. He did that by merging the most promising advances of the 1970s with new insights of his own, garnered and nurtured mainly from classroom experience.

David's first big success was the CES-70 chess team. He encouraged his students, underprivileged kids from the South Bronx of New York, to analyze through intelligently posed sets of logical examples. Solving problem after problem, the children soon developed the self-confidence to tackle increasingly complicated chess tasks. David's uncanny ability to tap inner talent motivated his students to achieve at levels few would have predicted. Not surprisingly, a high percentage of his pupils have relied on the analytical skills they assimilated under his tutelage to succeed in their college years and subsequent careers.

Soon thereafter David took his winning formula to Chess-in-the-Schools. His perspicacious evaluations and commitment to excellence helped shape that organization into the preeminent scholastic chess body in the country. Recently, David has brought his state-of-the-art methodology to the chess club at Dalton, one of the nation's outstanding private schools. Now David's stellar track record and his illuminating instructional videos, software, and mentoring books have paved the way for his latest offering, *The Chess Kid's Book of Checkmate*.

As the title indicates, the book is about checkmate. It spotlights conventional checkmates, how to execute them and how to create them. The key is the mating pattern, or the various ways pieces can give checkmate individually or in combination with other pieces. David contends that skill in chess is largely a matter of acquiring an arsenal of such winning patterns. He accordingly urges his students and readers to reinforce their understanding of these schematic templates by constant exercise and training, just as athletes and musicians practice certain moves or notes over and over.

David lays out his course in forty chapters. In each he defines a motif, offers examples, and, wherever desirable, provides clarifying explanation. Similar books often include unrelated or unnatural examples

that almost never occur in bona fide chess games, but David's demonstrations all make sense and have immediate practicality.

The forty chapters of *The Chess Kid's Book of Checkmate* are divided into five main sections. The first section deals with notation, terminology, checkmate definitions, and a distinguishing exposition of stalemate. David quite rightly presumes nothing. By familiarizing the reader in prefatory passages with terms such as escape square, focal point, battery, and double check, David avoids verbal obstacles that could otherwise stymie the reader's enjoyment and instructional journey.

The first significant group of checkmating weapons appears in part One. Here, David presents straightforward but compact dioramas that all of us must know, including some that can occur in the opening moves of a game. Part Two offers mixed mate in one move puzzles, where the problems can still be solved without a board, just by looking at the elucidating diagram. Part Three gives harder, but well-known paradigms that take longer to crack, yet remain solvable just by careful looking. And part Four delivers a cavalcade of memorable mating tactics played by the game's principal exponents.

Authentic checkmate stratagems are first offered in chapter 3, and the vital ones are all there, from support mate to smothered mate. As a rule, the concepts that follow are arranged primarily in blocks of four, going in graduated sequence from easiest to hardest, the way veteran chess teachers usually do it. Moreover, the student doesn't have to strain to find the answers: they're in smaller type right at the bottom of the same page. So there's no need to search out the correct replies on the next page, or hunt through the back of the book for chapter and number, or, worse yet, check answers by turning the book upside down.

Furthermore, David MacEnulty never lets words get in the way of what's to be learned. Indeed, *The Chess Kid's Book of Checkmate* is full of insights, anecdotes, history, and beautiful examples, all couched in the sort of language used by real students with real problems and real questions. David never employs abstract phraseology, nor does his book contain, as many didactic works do, terms that chess teachers themselves don't even use.

David's presentation is redolent with the wisdom that only the most experienced educators could possess. *The Chess Kid's Book of Checkmate* is a terrific teacher's manual because David MacEnulty is a terrific teacher. So whether you're trying to learn how to play or teach others, whether you're getting this book for yourself or someone else, you won't be disappointed. However often you turn to *The Chess Kid's Book of Checkmate*, you'll find yourself once again escorted through the wondrous world of chess by a guide who knows the way.

A Word of Advice to Kids
by Bruce Pandolfini

The best way to improve at chess is to play strong players as often as you can. The second best thing you can do is solve chess problems, and the best way to solve chess problems is in your mind, without moving the pieces on a real board. This takes a lot of practice, as well as patience, and the more practice you get, the more patient you'll become. Getting lots of practice and becoming really patient will eventually make you a winning player.

As you read through Mr. MacEnulty's excellent book, don't even take out a chessboard and pieces. Just look at the very clear diagrams in *The Chess Kid's Book of Checkmate* and go from there. Only after you've spent some time figuring things out in your head should you even bother to set up the positions with an actual chess set. If you do it the right way, trying to analyze the moves before playing them, without touching a single piece, you'll master the game long before it gets a chance to master you.

Good luck on your exciting adventure through David MacEnulty's *The Chess Kid's Book of Checkmate*. May chess always stay as challenging and as rewarding as he makes it for you in the pages of this delightful book.

Introduction

All checkmates have two things in common:

1) the King is under attack;
2) there is no way for the King to escape.

And this book is based on two big ideas.

The first big idea is that, since the ultimate goal of the game of chess is checkmate, the player who knows more about checkmate has an advantage over the player who knows less.

The second big idea comes naturally from the first: many checkmates fall into well-known patterns or ideas that can be studied and learned. Once they have been studied and learned, you can seamlessly incorporate these checkmate patterns in your own games.

While it is certainly possible—in fact, necessary—to discover new ideas over the board as you play, the player who remembers more patterns has an advantage over the player who has to make it all up on the spot.

What you don't know can cost you the game. Knowledge is power, and you get that power by studying. Studying checkmates helps you win games. It's that simple.

Since this is a beginner's book, the exercises start at a very basic level. Some students may find them very easy while others may find they have to think quite a bit on some of them. If you find them to be a little difficult at first, just go back and do them again. Athletes and musicians practice certain moves or exercises over and over. Each time you do an exercise, it gets easier and easier. That's because with each repetition the brain feels more and more familiar with the ideas it is learning. The more familiar you are with the ideas, the quicker you can achieve them on the board in actual play. In the chess player, the eye-brain coordination is essential to building pattern recognition. Skill in chess is largely a matter of training in pattern recognition.

If, on the other hand, you find the first exercises to be too easy, that's not a bad thing at all. The purpose is not necessarily to challenge the skill at this point. Rather, the goal (of the first part) is simply to present patterns that will be useful when playing games against real opponents. If you want to remember a pattern, seeing that pattern and then practicing it over and over is the best way to do it.

I recommend going through this book several times so you are able to quickly spot similar patterns in your own games.

In **PART ONE** of this book we are just building up pattern recognition. We first present a basic pattern, and then give a series of puzzles based on that pattern. We then move on to another pattern, and then another, until you have amassed a huge collection of checkmate patterns that can be used to win games.

In presenting the basic patterns, only the pieces needed to show the pattern are on the board. Most often there is only one King on the board simply because we don't want anything distracting us from seeing the most important idea, which is the basic pattern.

PART TWO is a collection of mixed mate-in-one-move puzzles. Once you know the basic patterns, the next step is to be able to recognize the patterns when you don't know ahead of time which one to look for. Part Two will give you practice in finding mate in a variety of situations.

PART THREE is made up of well-known patterns that take several moves to unfold. Each pattern is introduced with a brief history of how they came to be known. This section ends with a few mate-in-two or mate-in-three puzzles, randomly arranged so you can test your new skills in game situations.

PART FOUR is a look at how some of the great players of the game have found checkmate hidden in much more complicated positions. We do not give puzzles for this section, because this is, after all, a book for those just starting out, and expecting relative beginners to achieve the brilliance of Alekhine or Fischer is asking way too much. However, it is important for those just beginning to enjoy chess to know that this kind of magic can happen on the chessboard.

The final position in the book is taken from a student game where Chris Mayfield, at the time an 800 level fourth grade student from the Bronx, found an astonishing mate in three moves. Two masters at the tournament did not see it, yet Chris knew something was there. He spent twenty minutes studying the position before unleashing his deadly combination. His perseverance paid off, and is a good lesson to us all.

Chess Notation

Chess notation is simply the writing down of the moves. It's fairly easy, but it does take a little practice.

Naming the Squares

The chessboard is a square arrangement of sixty-four smaller squares, laid out in eight rows of eight squares each.

The rows going sideways are called **RANKS.** Ranks are numbered 1 through 8.

The rows going up and down the board are called **FILES.** Files are named after the first eight letters of the alphabet, a through h.

SQUARES are named after the file they are on *and* the rank they are on. Each square has only one name, which is made up of a letter and a number.

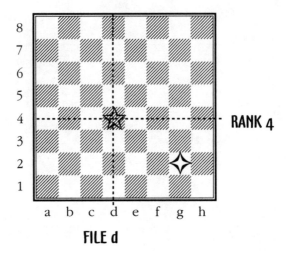

FILE d

As an example of how we name squares, the five-point star in this diagram is on the d-file and also on the 4th rank. So the star is on the square we call **d4**. The 'd' is a lower case letter, and the letter comes before the number.

We would not write this as D4, nor would we write it 4d. In chess we always name the file first, and it is always a lower case letter.

What square is the four-point star on?

Answer on top of next page.

The four-point star on the previous page is on g2.

Naming the Pieces

There are six different pieces in the chess army. Below are the names of the pieces, the symbol used in notation, and a picture of what it looks like on our diagrams.

Name	Symbol	Picture
King	K	♔
Queen	Q	♕
Rook	R	♖
Bishop	B	♗
Knight	N	♘
Pawn	P	♙

Note that we use only upper case letters as symbols for the pieces. That way there is no confusion between the upper case B for Bishop and the lower case b for the b-file.

You may have noticed that even though the word Knight is spelled with a 'K' as the first letter, we use the letter N as the symbol. That's because we need the letter K for the King.

Once you can name the squares and name the pieces by their symbol, you are ready to understand chess notation.

Writing the Moves

Although there are several ways to keep notation, we are only going to look at two of them here. These are the **Long Form Algebraic** and the **Short Form Algebraic.** Both are used in this book so you can become accustomed to both systems. Parts One and Two use the short form, while we use the long form in Parts Three and Four.

Short Form Algebraic

In the short form algebraic, we simply name the piece and the square it moves to. For example, if a Knight moves to f3, we write **Nf3**. If a Bishop moves to c4, we write **Bc4.**

For a Pawn move, we simply name the square the Pawn moves to. If no piece is designated, the unit moving is assumed to be a Pawn. For example, **e4** would indicate that a Pawn moved to the square e4. If it had been one of the pieces, say a Rook, there would have been an uppercase letter in front, as **Re4.**

If a piece or Pawn makes a capture, there is no special notation in the short form, although some people us the symbol "x" to show a capture.

For example, let's say a Bishop on b5 captures a Knight on c6. You could write this as either **Bc6** or **Bxc6.**

Long Form Algebraic

In the long form, we name the piece that is moving, the square it starts on, tell what it does, and name the square it moves to.

Let's take the example we just used of the Bishop on b5 capturing the Knight on c6. We would write that this way: **Bb5xc6.**

If we were to write that a Bishop moved from f1 to c4 without capturing anything, it would be **Bf1-c4.**

Here the dash means "moves to."

Pawn moves just name the starting square and the ending square, so if a Pawn moves from e2 to e4, we just write **e2-e4.** If there is no piece designated, then we assume the moving unit is a Pawn.

Long Form Algebraic gives a lot more information than the short form. Many chess teachers like the long form because, with the added information, they are more likely to be able to figure out what the moves actually are if their students make a mistake or two in the notation.

Numbering Moves

In order to keep track of the number of moves we have made, or to note which move we are on, each move is preceded by a number. So in the beginning of the game, **1. e4** in the short form algebraic would indicate that White's first move is the Pawn from e2 to e4.

In this book, the first move of each puzzle is given the designation "1." if it is White to move, and "1. ..." if it is Black to move.

Other symbols used in chess:

+	at the end of a move indicates that this move puts the opposing King in check.
++	at the end of a move indicates a double check.
#	at the end of a move indicates that this move gives checkmate.
0-0	is used to indicate castling on the Kingside, where there are two squares between the King and Rook.
0-0-0	is used to indicate castling on the Queenside, where there are three squares between the King and Rook.
1-0	means White wins.
0-1	means Black wins.
1/2-1/2	means the game is a draw.
!	indicates a strong move.
?	indicates a weak move or a mistake.
dis +	means there is a discovered check.
e.p.	indicates that there is an en passant capture.

Words and Terms to Know

Words stand for ideas. If you have a word for something, it means you know that idea. The more ideas you have, the more you can connect one idea to another, the smarter you are. In making checkmate, you have to know a lot of ideas, and chess players have a lot of neat words for those ideas. If you know the meanings of these words you can do a lot of checkmates.

SUPPORT

The first word is *support.* When something is *supported,* it is held up, backed, or assisted by something else. So in checkmates, if one piece is attacking the enemy King and is right next to the King, it must be *supported*—or protected—so the King cannot take it.

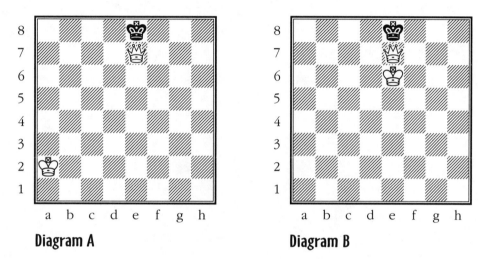

Diagram A   **Diagram B**

In Diagram A, the White Queen attacks the Black King, but she is not supported by anything. The Black King also attacks back!! The Black King can simply take the White Queen.

In Diagram B, however, the White Queen is *supported* by the King. This is the basic Support Mate (see p. 16).

FOCAL POINT

The next term we need to know is *focal point*. Actually, we have already used the idea for a *focal point*. A focal point is the square next to the enemy King that one of your pieces—usually the Queen—is going to occupy to give checkmate.

In Diagram C, the square e7 is the *focal point*. Since e7 is guarded by the White King, the White Queen can safely slide down the diagonal to e7 to deliver a support mate.

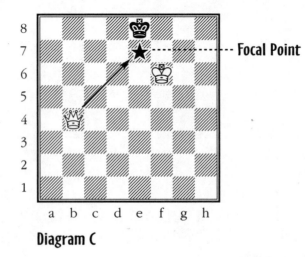

Diagram C

CONVERGE

To *converge* means to meet or to come together. In chess we often have two pieces attacking the same square from different directions. We say that the pieces *converge* on a particular square.

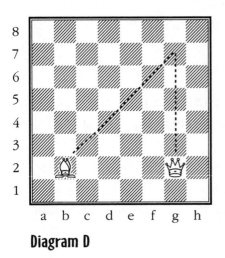

Diagram D

In Diagram D, the Bishop and Queen converge on the square g7. While this might not be important on an empty board, if there is a Black King on g8, as in Diagram E, then g7 becomes a focal point, and checkmate is in the air.

In Diagram E the convergence of the Bishop and Queen on g7 is fatal for Black.

Diagram F shows the final position. The White Bishop on b2 supports the White Queen for a checkmate on the focal point g7. The Queen simply runs up the file, captures the Pawn on g7, and that's a checkmate.

We write that as 1. Qxg7#.

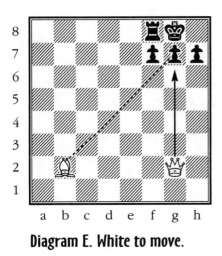

Diagram E. White to move.

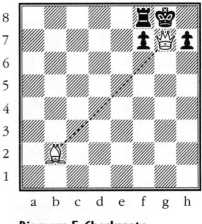

Diagram F. Checkmate.

BATTERY

A *battery* in the military refers to heavy artillery, and a battery in chess is the chess equivalent of a cannon. Two long-range pieces lined up together to attack along the same straight line is called a *battery,* and that can be a very powerful weapon. The battery in chess has the same effect as two pieces converging on the same square. The only differences are that in a battery the pieces come from the same direction, and they radiate their doubled power along the entire line of attack.

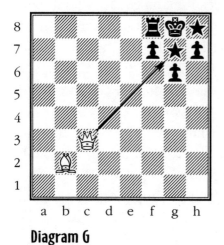

Diagram G

In Diagram G, the battery of the Bishop on b2 and the Queen on c3 attacks down the long diagonal. In this case there are two focal points: g7 and g8. Therefore, either 1. Qg7# or 1. Qh8# are the moves to make.

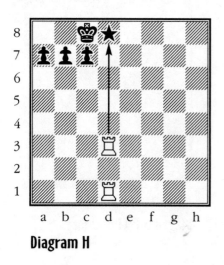

Diagram H

In Diagram H, the doubled Rooks on the d-file form a battery leading to the focal point d8. 1. Rd8#

ESCAPE SQUARES or FLIGHT SQUARES

An *escape square* or a *flight square* is a square to which the King can move to get out of check. If the King has an escape square, the check will not be mate.

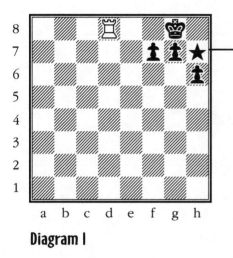

Here h7 is an *Escape* or *Flight Square*, so this is not checkmate.

Diagram I

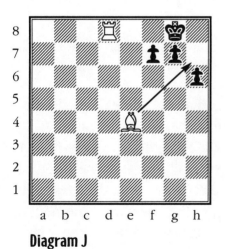

However, in Diagram J, the White Bishop on e4 takes away the escape square, so now we do have checkmate. The two White pieces *cooperate* (see p. 17) to get the mate.

Diagram J

ESCAPE FROM CHECK

There are three ways to escape from check. The King can **move (K)** out of the line of attack, you can **block** the check **(L)** by putting a piece in between the King and the attacker (unless the attacker is a Knight) or, best of all, you can **capture (M)** the attacking piece.

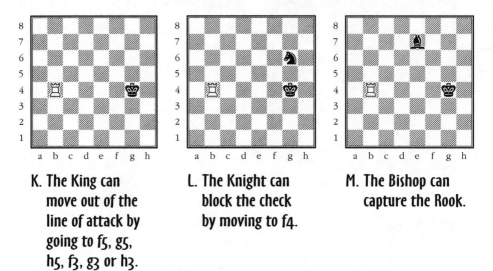

K. The King can move out of the line of attack by going to f5, g5, h5, f3, g3 or h3.

L. The Knight can block the check by moving to f4.

M. The Bishop can capture the Rook.

If you can't move, block, or capture, as in **Diagram N** below, then the position is **checkmate.**

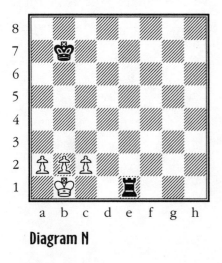

Diagram N

Here the White King is in check from the Black Rook on e1. If the White King tries to *move* to a1 or c1 it will still be in check. Pawns don't go backwards so nothing can *block* the check, and nothing can *capture* the Rook either.

If the King is in check and there is no way to move, block or capture, the position is *checkmate*. This is checkmate.

DOUBLE CHECK

In a *double check,* there is only one way to escape: the King must move. Blocking or capturing to stop one check still leaves the other in effect.

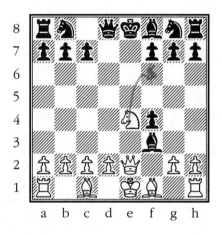

This position, for example, shows the great power of a double check.

White plays **1. Nf6!** with a double check that is also mate. The Knight attacks the King and at the same time takes away the potential flight square on d7, while the Queen on e2 now has a straight shot at the King down the open e-file.

Black seems to be able to capture either attacker, but whichever one Black takes, the check from the other is still in force.

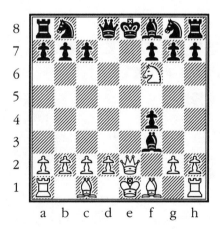

Not all double checks are fatal, but this one is. Taking the Knight still leaves check from the Queen, and taking the Queen still leaves the check from the Knight. **Checkmate!**

c h a p t e r

3

Types of Checkmate

Single-Piece Mates, Support Mates, Cooperative Mates, and Mating Patterns

Now that we have an understanding of chess notation, chess symbols, and some important words, it's time to look at how we classify checkmates.

In this book we classify and categorize checkmate patterns two ways. In the *first* system, we want to know if checkmate is given with one piece acting alone, or if one piece guards another that inflicts checkmate, or if one piece attacks the King while others prevent its escape.

We call these **single-piece mates, support mates** (or **helper mates**), and **cooperative mates.**

Types of Checkmate I

1. Single-Piece Mates: One piece checkmates the enemy King unassisted by others from his army.

For this to happen, at least one piece or Pawn from the checkmated King's army must block his escape.

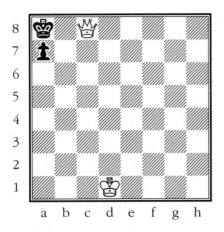

In the first example, the White Queen checkmates the enemy King with no help from any other White pieces.

The essential ingredients here are that the King is in the corner, so his space is already very limited, and the Black Pawn on a7 blocks the King's escape.

The second example shows the White King in a smothered mate from the Black Knight on f2.

Here the White King in the corner is completely hemmed in by its own pieces.

We call this pattern a Smothered Mate (see Chapter 36).

Types of Checkmate I (continued)

2. Support (or **Helper**) **Mate: one piece directly attacks the King, and is *supported* or guarded by another piece to prevent the King from capturing it.** Many people call this a *Helper Mate*.

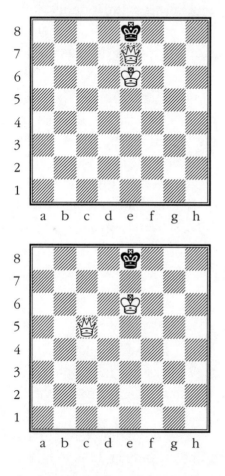

Here the White Queen gives checkmate *supported* by the White King.

Let's back this up one move.

The essential idea in the second diagram is that White has an attacker that can get to a checkmate square (e7) *and* a piece that is guarding that square (the King on e6).

In this case, e7 is a *focal point* for a checkmate.

The focal point is the square next to the enemy King that you will land on for checkmate. The checkmating piece must be *supported*. That's why we call these 'support mates.'

Alert readers will have noticed that the Queen could also go to c8 for checkmate. That is our theme on the next page.

Types of Checkmate I (continued)

3. The cooperative mate: two or more pieces combine to attack the King and take away all the King's escape squares.

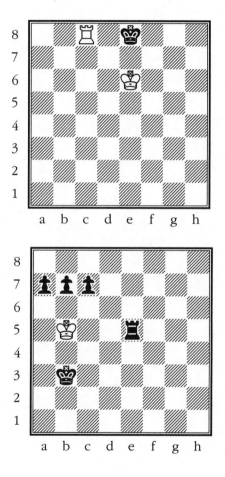

Here the White Rook attacks the Black King, taking away the entire eighth rank, and the White King keeps the Black King from escaping to the seventh rank.

The Rook and King *cooperate* to attack the King and take away all its escape squares.

Here the Black Rook attacks the White King, taking away the fifth rank. The Black King keeps the White King from escaping to the fourth rank, and the Black Pawns stop the King from escaping to the sixth rank.

The Rook, King, and Pawns *cooperate* to attack the King and take away all its escape squares.

The more ideas you have about checkmate, the more likely you are to see them during your games.

Types of Checkmate I (continued)

Naturally, there can also be a combination of ideas in one checkmate.

For example,

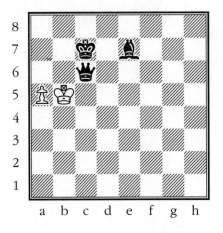

In this position, the Black Queen is on the focal point c6, supported by the Black King. The Black Queen takes away the sixth rank, the c-file, and the diagonal the White King is on. The Black Bishop cuts off b4, and the White Pawn blocks a5. So here we have a cooperative support mate where an escape square is blocked by a unit from the King's own army.

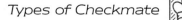

Types of Checkmate II
Checkmate Patterns

The *second* way we classify checkmates is by **patterns**. A pattern is something that recurs again and again, and the checkmate patterns shown in this book certainly do happen over and over. If you know the pattern, you can quickly go to the checkmate. If you don't know the pattern, you may miss a quick win.

Several years ago during a casual game in our chess room at school one of my students had a mate in one. He didn't see it. Neither did his opponent. That mate stayed on the board for two more moves. Then his opponent made a move that took away the mate in one, but now there was a forced mate in two. Neither player saw that either. Then the position moved back so the mate in one was there again. This went on for seven consecutive moves where one player had checkmate in either one or two moves. Eventually he actually lost the game.

More recently this position occurred, again in a casual game in the chess room.

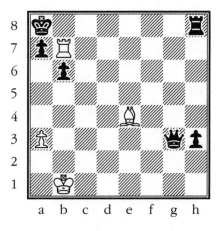

White had lost his Queen earlier, and saw an opportunity to get his opponent's Queen with a discovered check. He played 1. Rg7+, and took the Black Queen next move. After a series of not especially good moves by either side, the game ended in a draw.

But, had the player of the White pieces known his mating patterns, he would have seen **1. Rxb6#!** See chapter 14 for more on this pattern.

Stalemate

Stalemate occurs when the side to move is not in check, but has no legal moves. In a stalemate, nobody wins. The game is a tie or, as Chess players say, a **draw.**

Stalemate is the big enemy of the stronger side. In a tournament, each game is worth one point. If you win, you get the point and your opponent gets nothing. If you lose, your opponent gets the point and you get nothing. In a tie or draw, the two players split the point, so each person gets a half-point.

If you have enough pieces on the board to give checkmate and get a full point for the win, you certainly don't want to get a stalemate and settle for only half a point.

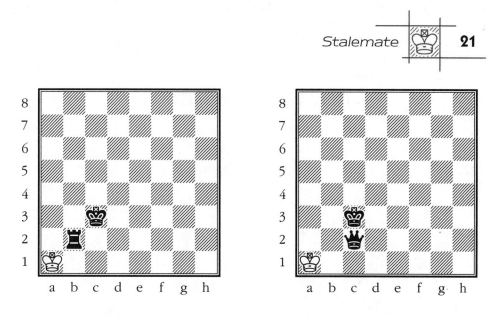

White to Move in both diagrams. Every move would put the White King in check, yet the White King is not now in check. White can't move in the first diagram because the Black Rook attacks a2 and b1, and the Rook on b2 is guarded by the Black King on c3. This is **stalemate.**

White can't move in the second diagram because the Black Queen on c2 attacks all the squares around the White King. The White King can't move into an attack on a2, b2 or b1. **Stalemate again.**

Even though Black is ahead by a Rook in the first diagram and a Queen in the second, these are both draws. Nobody wins and nobody loses. In either diagram if White had another piece that could move, it would not be a stalemate, because White would then have a legal move.

More Stalemate Patterns

In all the diagrams on this page, the side to move has no legal moves. Since every move would be check, every move is illegal. Since the King is not in check in any of these, **they are all stalemates.**

Black to move. Every move of the Black King is illegal.

Black to move. Every move of the Black King is illegal.

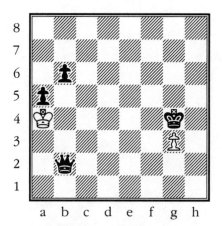

White to move. Every move of the White King is illegal, the White Pawn is blocked.

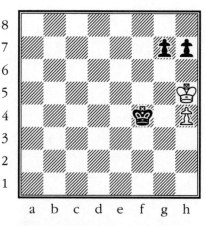

White to move. Every move of the White King is illegal, and the White Pawn is blocked.

Is it Checkmate, Stalemate, or Neither?

Study the following diagrams carefully. Determine if the position is checkmate, stalemate, or neither.

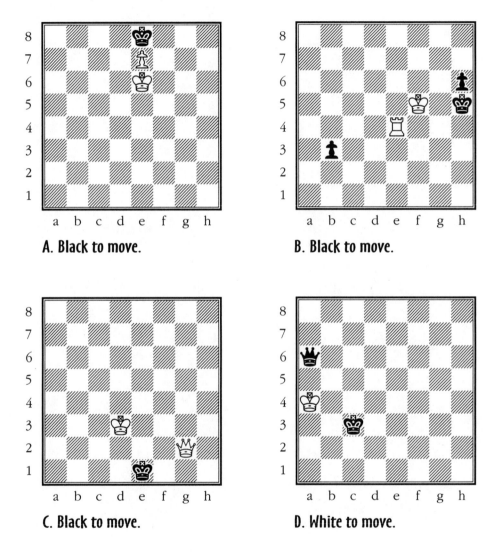

A. Black to move.

B. Black to move.

C. Black to move.

D. White to move.

Answers:
A. Stalemate. **B.** Neither. Black can move the Pawn on b3. **C.** Neither, but it should be checkmate on White's next move. **D.** Checkmate.

Part One

c h a p t e r
5

Checkmate in the Opening

The usual goals of the opening are to develop the pieces, control the center, and make sure the King is safe. Among reasonably experienced players, checkmate is not often on the mind in the first part of the game. However, it can be done, and every chess player should know about these ways of winning and losing quickly.

Scholar's Mate: Against a complete beginner, Scholar's Mate can end the game in just four moves.

In the initial set-up, the weakest squares on the board are f7 for Black and f2 for White. Only the King guards these two squares. In the Scholar's Mate, White targets f7 with a Bishop on c4 and a Queen on h5.

Experienced players will escape the danger easily. However, several years ago one of my students won his first sixteen tournament games with this little trick. With White or Black, he went after f7 or f2 with great determination. Since his opponents were just learning the game, he scored a steady stream of checkmates. Some of these wins took more than four moves, but by relentlessly targeting the weak squares f7 and f2 he was able to overpower his inexperienced opponents. Of course, then he started playing stronger opponents and discovered that scholar's mate is strictly for beginners. With no other weapons in his bag of tricks, he went on to lose a long string of games before he gave up his infatuation with the four move mate and learned to play chess properly. Although I strongly discourage students from trying this in tournaments, in the interest of being complete, here it is.

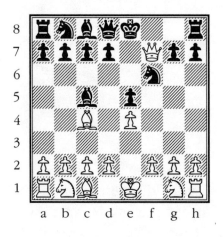

1.	e4	e5
2.	Bc4	Bc5
3.	Qh5	Nf6
4.	Qxf7# Diagram	

This is very easy to stop. After 2. Bc4, Black simply plays 2. ...Nf6!, and the White Queen can't get to h5 safely. If she does slide out to h5, her next checkmate will have to be in the next game, since the Knight on f6 will capture the Queen on h5.

The Two Move Mate

Yes, it is possible to win the game in just two moves. Your opponent has to play very badly, but it can be done.

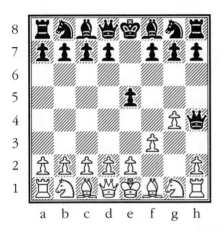

The moves of this catastrophe are

1. f3?   e5
2. g4???   Qh4#

This isn't an opening manual, but plainly White broke several principles of the opening in these two moves. He opened a line of attack to the King, didn't develop any pieces, and didn't do much about the center.

In case you think this can't happen in a real game, one of my first grade students actually won a game like this a the New York State Scholastic tournament.

The Three Move Mate

I have only seen this happen once, in a classroom game between an advanced beginner and a complete beginner.

1. e4   e5
2. Qh5? This isn't much of an attack, but as with the Scholar's Mate, against a beginner it has a chance of getting something. In this game, it got the King.
2. ...   Ke7??? The *only* move that loses immediately!
3. Qxe5#

A simple way to ward off this early attack by the White Queen is to simply guard the e5 Pawn with 2. ...Nc6.

Surprisingly the ideas in these quick wins can actually show up in real games. Here, for example, is a game alleged to have been played between two masters.

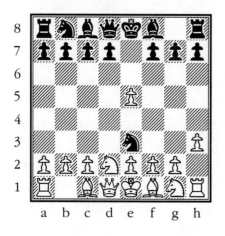

After

1.	d4	Nf6
2.	Nd2	e5
3.	dxe5	Ng4
4.	h3	Ne3!

White resigned. The Queen is trapped, and taking the Knight with

5. fxe3 leads to a six move variation of the two move mating pattern:

5.	...	Qh4+
6.	g3	Qxg3#

For more on checkmate in the opening, see Legal's Mate (Chapter 38) and Smothered Mate in the Opening (Chapter 36).

c h a p t e r

6

The Corridor, or
Back Rank, Mate

A *corridor* is a hall, with walls on both sides. You can easily see why this pattern is sometimes called a corridor mate. The King is stuck between the edge of the board and a wall of his own Pawns.

The King is also on its own back rank, so this is frequently called a *back rank mate.*

An enemy Queen or Rook sailing down to the last rank gives checkmate along the back rank. This example is a single-piece mate, but as we will see, many variations of the corridor mate require cooperation from other pieces. One example (puzzle #10) is also a support mate.

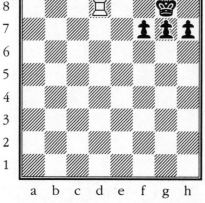

**Basic Pattern for the Corridor Mate,
also called the Back Rank Mate.**

When the King is stuck on the edge of the board and hemmed in by either his own pawns or by an attack from enemy pieces, there is a danger of some variation of the corridor or back rank mate.

The Corridor, or Back Rank, Mate (continued)

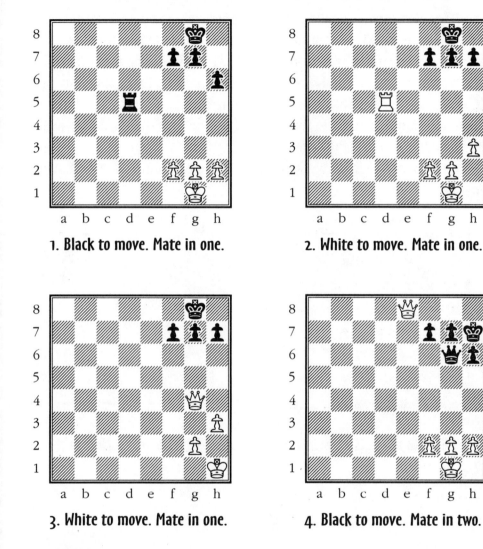

1. Black to move. Mate in one.

2. White to move. Mate in one.

3. White to move. Mate in one.

4. Black to move. Mate in two.

Solutions:

1) 1. ...Rd1#
2) 1. Rd8#
3) 1. Qc8#
4) 1 ...Qb1+; 2. Qe1, Qxe1#

The Corridor, or Back Rank, Mate (continued)

The Back Rank Mate is not always a matter of waiting for your opponent to leave his King unprotected. Most of the time you have to work at it to show that the back rank is weaker than your opponent thought. In diagram 5, Black's back rank is poorly protected. Black has only one defender on the eighth rank, while White has two attackers aimed at d8. In diagram 6, there are two defenders, but with the right first move White can drive one of the defenders back.

In Part IV of this book we will look at more elaborate ways of achieving a back rank mate.

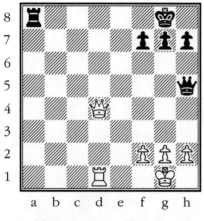

5. White to move. Mate in two.

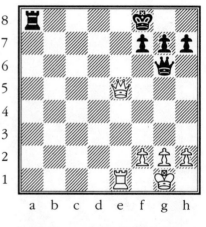

6. White to move. Mate in three.

Solutions:

5) 1. Qd8+, Rxd8; 2. Rxd8#

6) 1. Qe7+ forces the King back. 1. ... Kg8; 2. Qe8+, Rxe8; 3. Rxe8#

Variations on the Corridor Mate

Sometimes the wall that holds the King on the edge is made up of only one or two of its own Pawns. The other escape squares are under attack by enemy units.

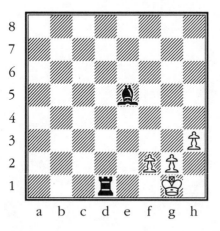

In this example, the White King is blocked on f2 and g2 by its own Pawns, but the Black Bishop on e5 attacks h2, preventing the King from escaping.

The Black Rook on d1 delivers checkmate because all the squares above the King are covered, thanks to the White Pawns on f2 and g2, and the cooperation of the Bishop's attack on h2. In this pattern, the Rook needed some help from his friend.

Variations on the Corridor Mate (continued)

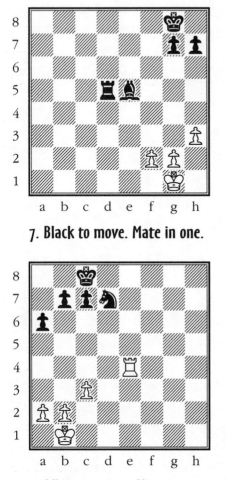

7. Black to move. Mate in one.

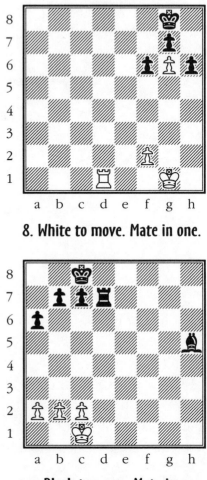

8. White to move. Mate in one.

9. White to move. Mate in one.

10. Black to move. Mate in one.

Solutions:

7) 1. ...Rd1#

8) 1. Rd8#

9) 1. Re8#

10) 1. ...Rd1#

Variations on the Corridor Mate (continued)

11. White to move. Mate in one.

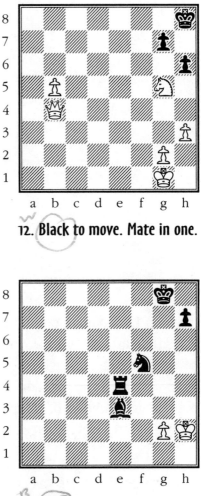

12. Black to move. Mate in one.

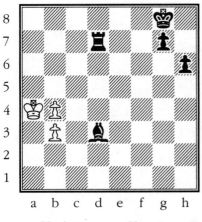

13. Black to move. Mate in one.

14. White to move. Mate in one.

Solutions:

11) 1. Qh5#
12) 1. Qf8#
13) 1. ...Ra7#
14) 1. ...Rh4#

chapter

7

Queen Checkmates

Because she attacks in eight different directions, and radiates power from one edge of the board to the other, the Queen is the most powerful piece on the board. Not surprisingly, she can give checkmate in more ways than any other piece. She also has more ways to both receive support and to cooperate with other pieces in inflicting checkmate.

In several of the corridor or back rank checkmates we have already seen some examples of the power of the Queen. The following pages show even more of the great power and versatility of the Queen.

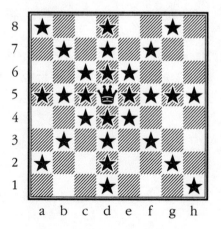

Queen Checkmate Patterns

1st Basic Pattern of the Queen Checkmate.

2nd Basic Pattern of the Queen Checkmate.

3rd Basic Pattern of the Queen Checkmate (also called an Epaulettes Mate).

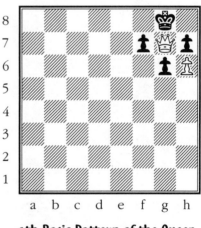

4th Basic Pattern of the Queen Checkmate.

Queen Checkmate Problems

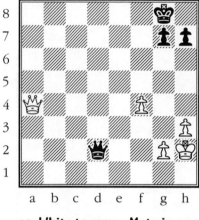

15. White to move. Mate in one.

16. White to move. Mate in one.

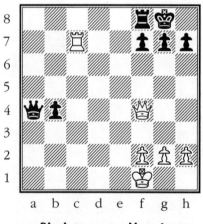

17. Black to move. Mate in one.

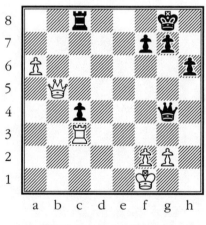

18. Black to move. Mate in one.

Solutions:
15) 1. Qe8#
16) 1. Qh7#
17) 1. ...Qd1#
18) 1. ...Qd1#

Queen Checkmate Problems (continued)

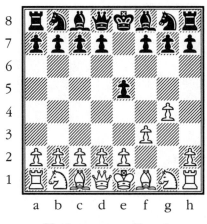

19. Black to move. Mate in one.

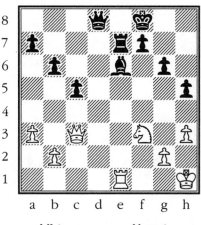

20. White to move. Mate in one.

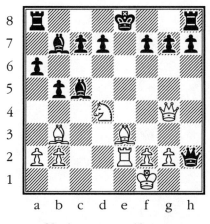

21. Black to move. Mate in one.

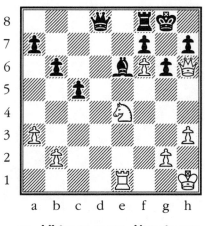

22. White to move. Mate in one.

Solutions:
19) 1. ...Qh4#
20) 1. Qh8#
21) 1. ...Qh1#
22) 1. Qg7#

Queen and Rook Checkmates

The Queen and Rook are the two most powerful pieces on the board. However, on an otherwise empty board, even they like to have the opposing King on the edge of the board.

Here the White Queen attacks the Black King on the eighth rank while the White Rook stands guard on the seventh rank, preventing the Black King from escaping. When there are open ranks near the enemy King, the cooperation between these two powerful pieces can be unstoppable.

In other patterns with these two powerful pieces one piece gives mate while the other protects or supports the attacking piece, as in patterns two, three, and four on the next page.

Queen and Rook Checkmate Patterns

The Queen and Rook are the two most powerful pieces on the board. However, on an otherwise empty board, even they like to have the opposing King on the edge of the board.

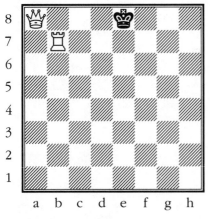

1st Basic Pattern for the Queen and Rook Checkmate.

2nd Basic Pattern for the Queen and Rook Checkmate.

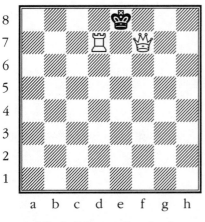

3rd Basic Pattern for the Queen and Rook Checkmate.

4th Basic Pattern for the Queen and Rook Checkmate.

Queen and Rook Checkmate Problems

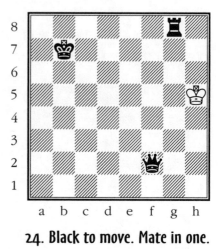

23. Black to move. Mate in one.

24. Black to move. Mate in one.

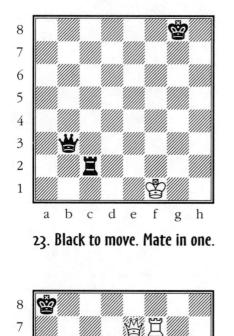

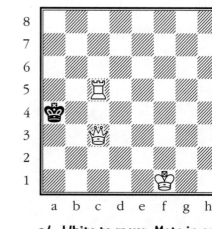

25. White to move. Mate in one.
Six solutions.

26. White to move. Mate in one.

Solutions:
23) 1. ...Qb1#
24) 1. ...Qh2#
25) 1. Qa7#, 1. Qb7#, 1. Qd8#, 1. Qe8#, 1. Qf8#, and 1. Rf8#
26) 1. Ra5#

Queen and Rook Checkmates (continued)

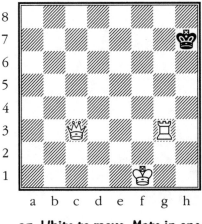

27. White to move. Mate in one.

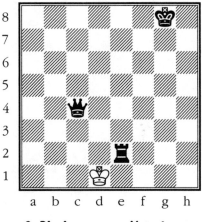

28. Black to move. Mate in one.

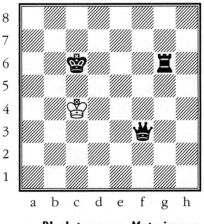

29. Black to move. Mate in one.

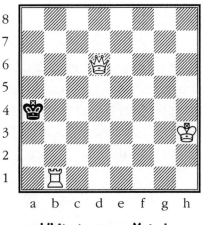

30. White to move. Mate in one. Two Solutions.

Solutions:

27) 1. Qg7#

28) 1. ...Qc2#

29) 1. ...Rg4#

30) 1. Qb4# and 1. Qa6#

Queen and King
Checkmates

The Big Idea in the Queen and King Checkmate is that the lone King has been driven to the edge, and the strong side's King and Queen cooperate to deliver mate. The Queen gives check while her King helps to keep the opposing King from getting off the edge. In some cases, such as the One-Two-Three mate shown below, the strong side's King also supports or protects the Queen.

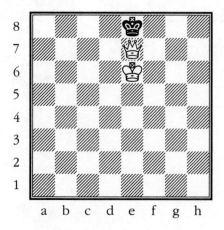

This is an essential checkmate for all chessplayers to know. The first thing we will learn is the different patterns for checkmate. Then we will learn how to chase the King to the edge of the board so the checkmate can be done.

You should win every game—no stalemates—when you have the advantage of a Queen and King to a lone King.

Queen and King Checkmate Patterns

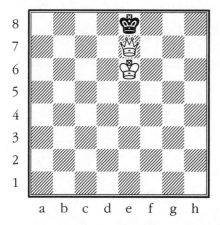

1st Basic Pattern for the King and Queen Checkmate (sometimes called the One-Two-Three Checkmate, or the Queen Sandwich).

2nd Basic Pattern for the King and Queen Checkmate (sometimes called the Right Angle Checkmate).

3rd Basic Pattern for the King and Queen Checkmate.

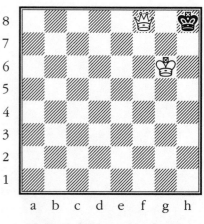

4th Basic Pattern for the King and Queen Checkmate.

More Queen and King Mating Patterns

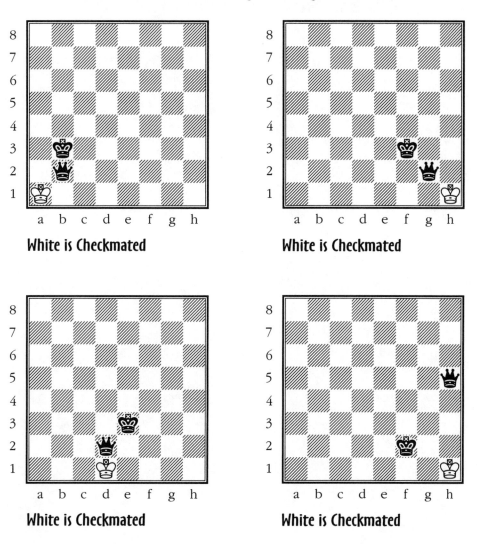

White is Checkmated

White is Checkmated

White is Checkmated

White is Checkmated

Not Checkmate

When just learning this checkmate, many people make basic errors in judgment. The positions in the diagrams below have all occurred in real games. The strong side mistakenly thought these were checkmate.

How can the King escape in the following diagrams?

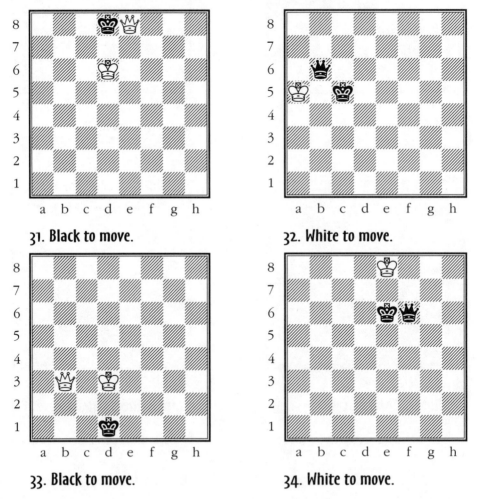

31. Black to move.

32. White to move.

33. Black to move.

34. White to move.

Solutions:

31) 1. ...Kxe8
32) 1. Ka4
33) 1. ... Ke1 or 1. ...Kc1
34) White can't move. This is stalemate, not checkmate.

Queen and King Checkmate Problems

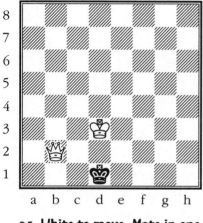

35. White to move. Mate in one. Three solutions.

36. White to move. Mate in one. Two solutions.

37. Black to move. Mate in one.

38. Black to move. Mate in one.

Solutions:
35) 1. Qa1#, 1. Qb1# and 1. Qd2#
36) 1. Qd2# and Qf1#
37) 1. ...Qb6#
38) 1. ...Qh4#

Queen and King Checkmate Problems (continued)

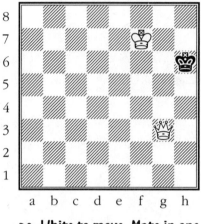

39. White to move. Mate in one. Two solutions.

40. White to move. Mate in one. Two solutions.

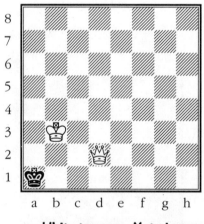

41. White to move. Mate in one. Five solutions.

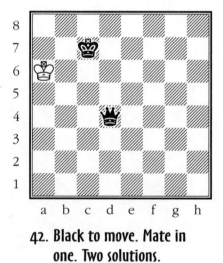

42. Black to move. Mate in one. Two solutions.

Solutions:

39) 1. Qg6# and 1. Qh4#
40) 1. Qa7# and 1. Qa1#
41) 1. Qa2#, 1. Qb2#, 1. Qc1#, 1. Qd1# and 1. Qe1#
42) 1. ...Qb6# and 1. ...Qa4#

Checkmate with the Queen and King

Checkmate with a King and Queen is a very important skill for every chess player to develop.

If you are down to just a King and Pawn against a King, and you manage to promote the Pawn (see *The Chess Kid's Book of the King and Pawn Endgame*), suddenly you have a King and Queen against a King. *You absolutely must know how to win this ending.*

Now that we have seen the final positions for the King and Queen checkmate, let's see how we can force them from the worst possible position: the lone King in the middle of the board, and the attacking King and Queen on the edge.

Because the Queen is so powerful, she can actually drive the enemy King to the edge of the board. No other piece acting alone can do that.

Knight's Jump Away System

There are several ways to force checkmate with a King and Queen, but we are going to focus on just one of them: The Knight's Jump Away System. There are four steps to this checkmate. An interesting thing about the system we are going to use here is that the Queen will not actually check the King until the final checkmate position is reached.

Step One: Move the Queen as close to the opposing King as possible without giving check or getting taken. This will be the distance of a Knight's jump.

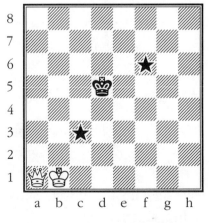

And now it's time for step two.

In this position, the Queen moves to either c3 or f6.

In almost any random placement of these three pieces, the Queen will be able to move to a Knight's jump away from the King in one move. In a few cases it may take two moves.

Let's play :

1. Qc3! (Qf6 is also good).

Checkmate with the Queen and King (continued)

Step Two: Follow the King to the edge of the board. In this, the longest part of the system, the Queen will simply do everything the opposing King does. If the King moves up his file, she moves up her file. If the King moves down a diagonal, the Queen moves down a diagonal, always moving in the same direction and always staying a Knight's jump away. She just shadows every move of the King.

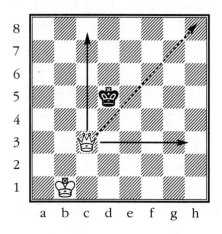

Position after 1. Qc3, a Knight's jump away from the King.

The dark arrows show that the King is in a box. The sides of the box are the eighth rank, the h-file, and the walls the Queen has put up from c3 to c8, and from c3 to h3.

Right now the Black King has twenty-five squares to move on. As the Queen follows the King, his space gets smaller and smaller, until finally, he will only have two or three squares on the edge of the board.

The King moved from d5 to e4 sliding down the diagonal. The Queen does exactly the same thing, sliding down her diagonal:

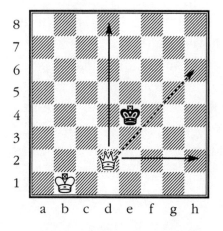

1. ...   Ke4
2. Qd2!

The King now has twenty four squares in the box (we are ignoring the diagonal attack of the Queen here; it's the outside of the box that matters).

Checkmate with the Queen and King Step Two (continued)

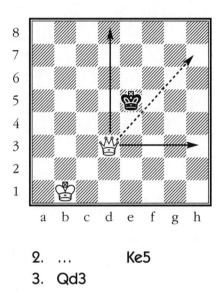

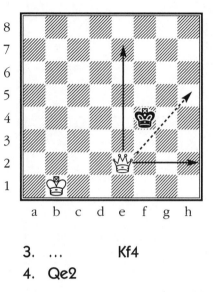

2. ...	Ke5		3. ...	Kf4
3. Qd3			4. Qe2	

The King moved up the e-file, so the Queen moves up the d-file. Now the King has only twenty squares.

The King moved down the diagonal, so the Queen moves down the diagonal. It's as if they were wheels on a car. What one does, the other does. The King is losing more space. He's down to just eighteen squares.

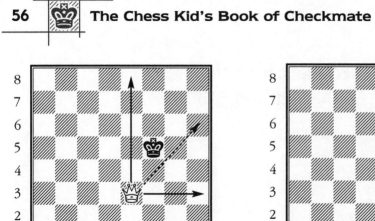

4. ...	Kf5
5. Qe3	

Down to just fifteen squares.

5. ...	Kg4
6. Qf2	

Twelve squares in the box. The King has been doing his best not to get to the edge of the board, but it's no use. The Queen is too powerful.

Checkmate with the Queen and King Step Two (continued)

The Black King naturally wants to avoid the edge of the board. Let's jump ahead three moves, and look at the position where Black is about to hide in the corner.

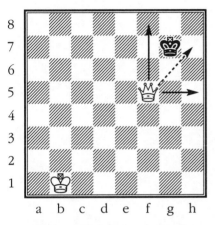

Black's best move is to get in the corner and hope White makes a mistake.

What is the mistake Black is hoping for? *Black hopes White will continue to follow him! Qg6 is a blunder!*

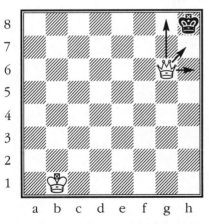

This is Stalemate. Do Not Follow the King into the Corner!

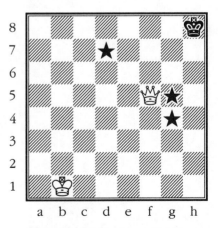

Instead, White moves to any of the starred squares. Queen to d7, g5, or g4 all leave Black room to move so there is no stalemate.

Checkmate with the Queen and King (continued)

Step Three: Call for help. At this point, the Queen has done all she can do alone. She has forced the King to the edge, and now she stands guard to keep him from leaving the edge. It's time to ask her King to come help out. Without the support of the King, all the White Queen can do is stand and watch the Black King move back and forth, or move in for a stalemate, neither of which is very sensible. So while the Black King wanders back and forth on his two or three squares on the edge of the board, the White King makes his way over to support the Queen.

His target square is f6, because from there, he supports the Queen for checkmate no matter whether the Black King is on h8, h7, or h6.

Step Four: Deliver the checkmate!

Qg7#.

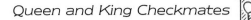

Queen and King Checkmate Problems

Find the best move. In the last pursuit of the King, we showed the best moves by Black as the King tried to avoid the edge of the board. Sometimes your opponent is not so difficult, and mistakenly heads for the edge on purpose. *When the enemy King is on any of the four edges of the board, the strong side's Queen should immediately take over the row of squares next to the King, always making sure the position is not stalemate.* Then bring up the friendly King and make checkmate.

In diagram **O** below, White should immediately play **1. Qg4!**, locking the King down on the h-file. **Find the best moves in the remaining three diagrams.**

Diagram O

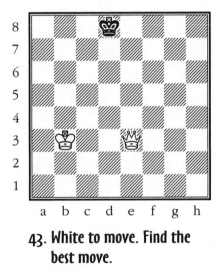

43. White to move. Find the best move.

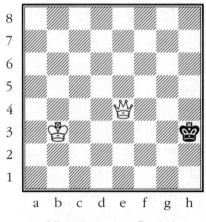

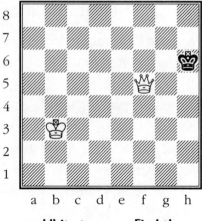

44. White to move. Find the best move.

45. White to move. Find the best move.

Solutions:
43) 1. Qa7
44) 1. Qg6
45) 1. Qg4

Queen Checkmates: The Swallow's Tail Pattern

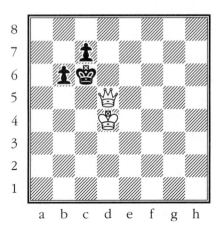

Pattern #1 A Queen attacking the enemy King from an adjacent square on the diagonal always leaves two flight squares for the King. These two flight squares resemble a swallow's tail, giving this pattern its name. In this diagram, Black is blocked from the escape squares by his own Pawns. It doesn't matter what prevents the King from escaping, as long as something does. For example, if the Black Pawns were missing, a White Knight on a8 or a Bishop on a5 or d8 would accomplish the same thing. There are many other ways of taking away the flight squares.

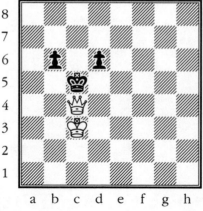

Pattern #2 A Queen attacking the enemy King from an adjacent square on the rank or file also leaves two flight squares for the King. In this diagram, Black is again blocked from the escape squares by his own Pawns. Here again, if the Black Pawns were not there, a White Knight on c8 or a Rook on the sixth rank would accomplish the same thing. There are many other ways of taking away the flight squares.

More Swallow's Tail Patterns

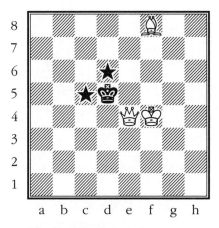

Black is checkmated.
The Bishop takes away the
escape squares c5 and d6.

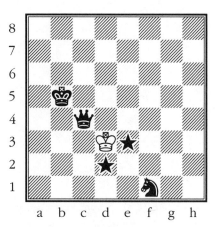

White is checkmated.
The Knight takes away the
escape squares d2 and e3.

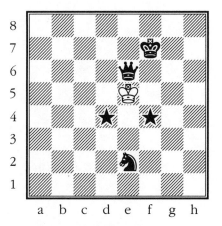

White is checkmated.
The Knight takes away the escape
squares d4 and f4.

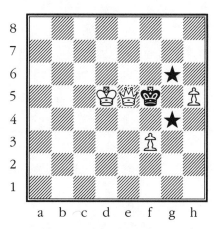

Black is checkmated.
The Pawns take away the
escape squares g4 and g6.

Swallow's Tail Checkmate Problems

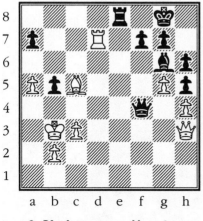

46. Black to move. Mate in one.

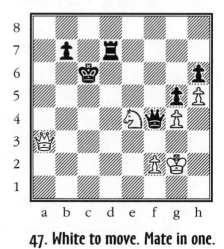

47. White to move. Mate in one.

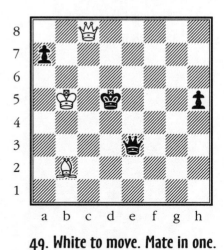

48. Black to move. Mate in one.

49. White to move. Mate in one.

Solutions:
46) 1. ...Qd6#
47) 1. Qc5#
48) 1. ...Qa4#
49) 1. Qc6#

Swallow's Tail Checkmate Problems

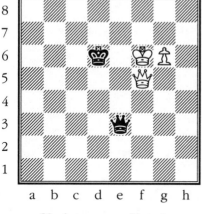

50. Black to move. Mate in one.

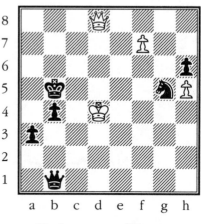

51. Black to move. Mate in one.

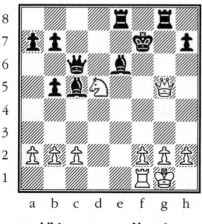

52. White to move. Mate in one.

53. White to move. Mate in one.
Black to move. Mate in one.

Solutions:
50) 1. ...Qe7#
51) 1. ...Qe4#
52) 1. Qf6#
53) White: 1. Qd6#; Black: 1. ...Qh2#

Queen and Bishop
Checkmates

When the Queen teams up with the Bishop, we get another set of patterns that every chess player should know. With the Queen's ability to give checkmate up close *and* from a distance, some surprising patterns can emerge when her partner strikes along the diagonals.

The Bishop can hide in a far corner while protecting the Queen for a checkmate or, as in the diagram below, deliver the blow himself while the Queen covers all the remaining escape squares.

Queen and Bishop Checkmate Patterns

The Bishop and Queen can checkmate in many different ways. Every chess player should be familiar with the following patterns.

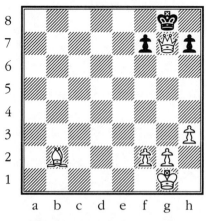

1st Basic Pattern of the Queen and Bishop Checkmate.

2nd Basic Pattern of the Queen and Bishop Checkmate.

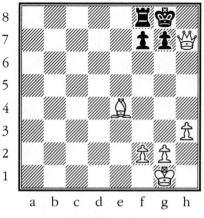

3rd Basic Pattern of the Queen and Bishop Checkmate.

4th Basic Pattern of the Queen and Bishop Checkmate.

Queen and Bishop Checkmate Problems

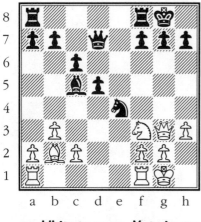

54. White to move. Mate in one.

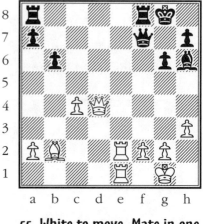

55. White to move. Mate in one.

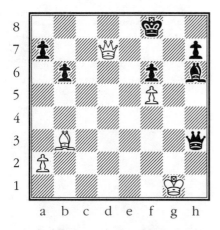

56. White to move. Mate in one.
Black to move. Mate in one.

57. Black to move. Mate in one.

Solutions:

54) 1. Qxg7#
55) 1. Qh8#
56) White: 1. Qf7#; Black: 1. ...Be3#
57) 1. ...Qf2#

Queen and Bishop Checkmate Problems (continued)

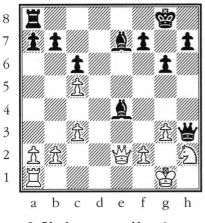

58. Black to move. Mate in one.

59. Black to move. Mate in one.

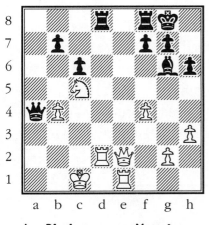

60. Black to move. Mate in one.

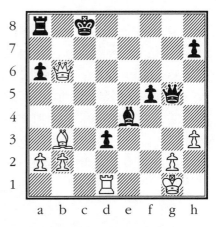

61. White to move. Mate in one. Black to move. Mate in one.

Solutions:

58) 1. …Qg2#

59) 1. …Qh1#

60) 1. …Qa1#

61) White: 1. Be6#; Black: 1. …Qxg2#

Queen and Knight Checkmates

With the peculiar leap of the Knight on her side, the Queen gains yet another set of checkmate patterns. The Queen and Knight are a very dangerous combination, since the Knight is the only piece whose moves are not at all like the Queen's. When they team up, with the Knight's ability to reach around a corner and the Queen's formidable power on ranks, files, and diagonals, a nearby King is often in grave danger, as can be seen from the diagram below.

Queen and Knight Checkmate Patterns

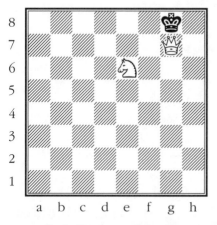

1st Basic Pattern of the Queen and Knight Checkmate.

2nd Basic Pattern of the Queen and Knight Checkmate.

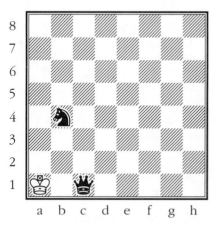

3rd Basic Pattern of the Queen and Knight Checkmate.

4th Basic Pattern of the Queen and Knight Checkmate.

Queen and Knight Checkmate Problems

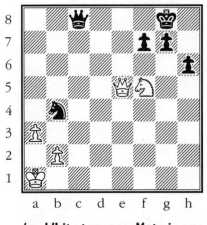

62. White to move. Mate in one.
    Black to move. Mate in one.

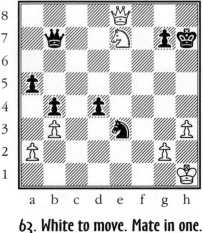

63. White to move. Mate in one.
    Black to move. Mate in one.

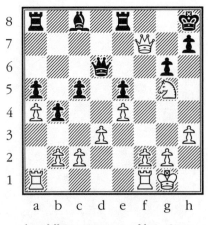

64. White to move. Mate in one.

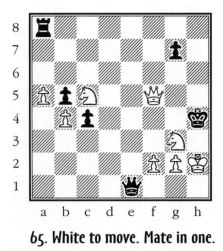

65. White to move. Mate in one.

Solutions:

62) White: 1. Qxg7#; Black: 1. ...Qc1#
63) White: 1. Qh5#; Black: 1. ...Qxg2#
64) 1. Qxh7#
65) 1. Qh5#

Queen and Knight Checkmate Problems (continued)

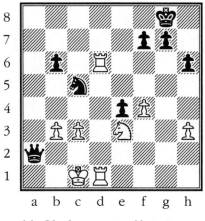

66. Black to move. Mate in one.

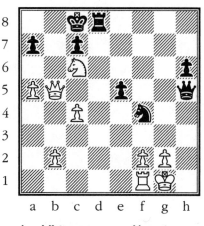

**67. White to move. Mate in one.
Black to move. Mate in one.**

68. White to move. Mate in one.

**69. White to move. Mate in one.
Black to move. Mate in one.**

Solutions:

66) 1. ...Nxb3#
67) White: 1. Nxa7# or 1. Ne7#; Black 1. ...Ne2#
68) 1. Ng6#
69) White: 1. Qxa3#; Black: 1. ...Qc1#

Queen and Knight Checkmate Problems (continued)

70. Black to move. Mate in one.

71. White to move. Mate in one.

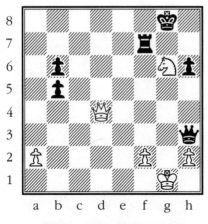

72. White to move. Mate in one.

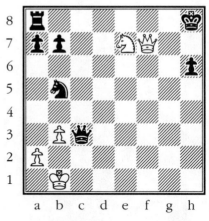

73. White to move. Mate in one.
Black to move. Mate in one.

Solutions:
70) 1. ...Ng4#
71) 1. Qd6#
72) 1. Qh8#
73) White: 1. Ng6#; Black: 1. ...Na3#

King and Rook
Checkmates

Along with the Queen and King Checkmate, the checkmate with the King and Rook is an absolutely essential skill for every chess player to master. The good news is that if you know the technique, *you will win this position every time, no matter who you are playing.*

We will begin with what the final pattern looks like, then show ways to force that final pattern when you are only two moves away, and finally learn how to force the checkmate when the King starts out in the middle of the board.

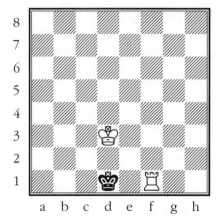

1st Basic Pattern of the King and Rook Mate.

2nd Basic Pattern of the King and Rook Mate. When the King is in the corner, the strong side's King does not have to be directly over it; the edge of the board keeps the King from escaping.

The three key elements here are:

(1) the lone King is stuck on the edge;

(2) the strong side's King stands over the lone King, preventing it from getting off the edge; and

(3) the strong side's Rook is able to checkmate the lone King on the edge.

King and Rook Checkmate Problems

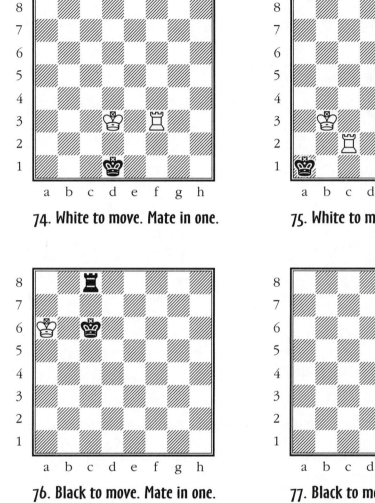

74. White to move. Mate in one.

75. White to move. Mate in one.

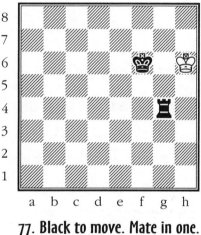

76. Black to move. Mate in one.

77. Black to move. Mate in one.

Solutions:

74) 1. Rf1#
75) 1. Rc1#
76) 1. ...Ra8#
77) 1. ...Rh4#

King and Rook Checkmate Techniques

Now that we know what mate in one looks like, let's look at a few tricks we need to know to force the mate.

Technique #1: the Cut-Off

The Black King is on the edge of the board with three squares to move to: d1, f1, and f2.

White wants the Black King on d1. because then the White King would be holding the Black King down on rank one.

Naturally, Black wants no part of that. Black wants to go to f1 or f2. If White can block f1 and f2, Black's only move will be to d1. Therefore, **1. Rf3!**, *cutting off* the Black King's escape to the f-file.

   1. ...   **Kd1** the only move.

   2. Rf1#

This time the White King is on the edge, again with three choices: b8, b7, and d8. Black wants the White King on d8, so a simple cut-off, taking away the b-file, is the solution.

   1. ...   **Rb5!** Cutting off the White King's escape to the b-file and chasing it back to d8.

   2. Kd8 allowing Black to finish off with

   2. ...   **Rb8#**

King and Rook Checkmate Techniques (continued)

Technique #2: the Pull Back

The Black King on the edge of the board is about to take the White Rook.

To make a checkmate, White needs to both save the Rook and force the Black King to d1, where the White King would be holding the Black King down on rank one.

Therefore,

1. Rf3!, a pull-back, both saving the Rook and stopping the Black King's escape to the f-file. The Rook could also have pulled back to f4, f5, f6, f7, or f8 and still gotten the mate on the next move.

1. ...   **Kd1** the only move.

2. Rf1#

Note that on the first move, moving the Rook along the second rank would not force mate on the next move. The King could escape to f1.

Here again the lone King threatens the Rook. This time, however, the pull-back is along the rank not the file.

1. ...   **Rc7!** (or d7, e7, f7, g7, or h7) and White has only one move:

2. Ka5 allowing Black to finish off with

2. ...   **Ra7#**

These two techniques, the cut-off and the pull-back, can also be used in the middle of the board as ways of forcing the lone King to back up toward one of the edges.

King and Rook Checkmate Problems

Let's practice these two techniques.

78. White to move. Mate in two.

79. Black to move. Mate in two.

80. Black to move. Mate in two.

81. White to move. Mate in two.

Solutions:

78) 1. Re4, Kh6; 2. Rh4#

79) 1. ...Rd6 (or d5, d4, d3, d2, or d1); 2. Kf8, Rd8#

80) 1. ...Rc5; 2. Ke1; Rc1#

81) 1. Rc4 (or d4, e4, g4, or h4), Ka6; 2. Ra4#

King and Rook Checkmate Techniques (continued)

Before we learn to chase the lone King to the edge of the board so we can get one of these King and Rook checkmates, let's look at two other very important techniques, the **King Face-Off** and the **Box**.

The King Face-Off

The position below in Diagram P is a **King Face-Off.** The two Kings stand toe to toe, each keeping the other from moving to the fourth rank. If White now plays **1. Rb5**, the lone King will be driven back to the sixth rank. Black has three choices:

A) If Black moves to c6, attacking the Rook, White *does not retreat the Rook.* Instead, he simply moves the King to c4, guarding the Rook.

B) If Black moves to d6, White advances *diagonally* to e4. Then the Black King will either have to go to e6, for another King face-off, or to c6, allowing the Rook to **put him in a box** (Diagram next page).

C) If Black moves to e6, White advances *straight forward* to d4 where again Black can come back to d6 for another King Face-Off, or move further to the side to f6, again allowing the Rook to slide over to e5 for another box on the other side of the board.

Diagram P

This is an important position in these endings. The two Kings are opposing each other, neither permitting the other to advance.

When two Kings face off like this it is called the Opposition, because the two Kings oppose one another, each preventing the other from making forward progress.

Here the Rook check on b5 **drives back** the lone King. So we could also call this a *drive-back* position.

King and Rook Checkmate Techniques (continued)

The Box

We make a box by posting a protected Rook near the lone King. By drawing an imaginary line from the Rook along the Rank and File to the edges of the board, and using the two edges of the board for the remaining walls of the box, we completely enclose the King in a box.

Once you have the lone King in a box, on every move you either make the box smaller by moving in with the Rook, or you improve the position of your King.

Once you have put the King in the box, don't let it out!

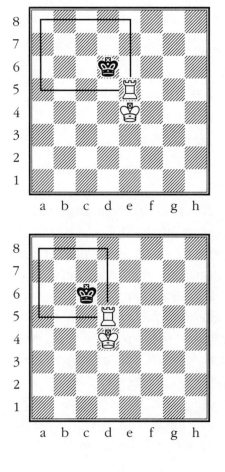

In this position, for example, the lone King is enclosed in the box shown by the lines.

White to move cannot do any better with the Rook. 1. Rd5+ would be a mistake because that would permit the lone King to escape to e6. Since moving the Rook is bad, we move the King in.

1. Kd4 Black has only three moves with the King. Two—d7 and c7—put it on the seventh rank, so Black tries

1. ...   Kc6

White now moves one wall of the box in.

2. Rd5! (second diagram) The box just got smaller and Black lost three more squares of roaming territory.

The Black King again has only three squares to move to, and all three put it one square from the edge.

If Black tries 2. ...Kb6, White pushes the wall in further with 3. Rc6.

If Black tries 2. ...Kc7, White moves in with the King: 3. Kc5

If Black tries 2. ...Kb7, White closes in from above: 3. Rd6.

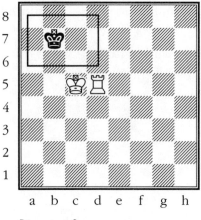

Diagram Q

Let's say Black picks

2. ... Kc7
3. Kc5 Kb7 Diagram Q.

Black stays off the edge as long as possible. But now the walls come tumbling down on top of the lone King.

4. Rd7+! Every move of the Black King is to one of the edges of the board.

You might think that the square a6 is not really part of the box, since it is not under attack. Does it give the Black King a chance to escape? No! In fact, moving to a6 gives White a quick mate, as we will see below.

If

4. ... Ka6
5. Rc7 Ka5
6. Ra7#

If

4. ... Ka8
5. Kb6 Kb8
6. Rd8#

If

4. ... Kb8
5. Kb6 Kc8
6. Rd6 Kb8
7. Rd8#

If

4.	...	Kc8
5.	Kc6	Kb8
6.	Kb6	Kc8 (6. ...Ka8; 7. Rd8#)
7.	Rd6	Kb8
8.	Rd8#	

Checkmate with the King and Rook

Now lets look at all these ideas—the cut-off, the pull-back, the King face-off, and the box—in action, as we drive the lone King to the edge of the board for a forced checkmate.

Unlike the Queen, the Rook cannot chase the King to the edge of the board without the aid of the King. Since the King is so slow, we begin by getting it close to the action.

Step One: Bring up the King for a King Face-Off.

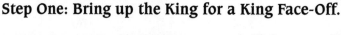

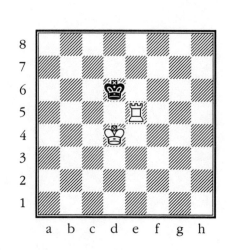

1. Kb2	**Kd4** Black keeps

the King in the middle as long as possible.

2. Kc2	**Ke4**
3. Kc3	**Kd5**

Now White can use the cut-off to chase the lone King into a face-off position.

4. Re1!	**Kc5**

And now White drives the lone King back one more rank with

5. Re5+	**Kd6**
6. Kd4	(Diagram) Guarding the

Rook. Now the lone King is in a box.

6. ...   **Kc6** Black stays as far from the edge as possible.

7. Rd5 moving in one wall of the box.

7. ...	**Kb6**
8. Rc5	**Kb7**

    9. Kd5 White cannot safely move in one of the walls with the Rook, so he improves the position of the King.

    9. ...   **Kb6** staying off the edge.

    10. Kd6 still improving the King's position.

    10. ...   **Kb7**

    11. Rb5+! And at last the lone King will be on one of the edges of the board.

Checkmate with the King and Rook (continued)

Position after 11. Rb5+

Black has four moves, and they all lead to checkmate.

A)

11.	...	Ka6
12.	Kc6	Ka7
13.	Ra5+	Kb8
14.	Ra6 The pull-back.	
14.	...	Kc8
15.	Ra8#	

B)

11.	...	Ka7
12.	Kc7	Ka6
13.	Rc5 another pull-back	
13.	...	Ka7
14.	Ra5#	

C)

11.	...	Ka8
12.	Kc7 forcing a face-off.	
12.	...	Ka7
13.	Ra5#	

D)

11.	...	Kc8
12.	Rb6 yet another pull-back.	
12.	...	Kd8
13.	Rb8#	

c h a p t e r

14

Rook and Bishop Checkmate

The Bishop and Rook frequently pair up to force checkmate, but there is always at least one square the two of them cannot cover (in some positions, it's more than one). Quite often an enemy Pawn cuts off its own King's flight square, as in the diagram below.

Rook and Bishop Checkmate Patterns

1st Basic Pattern of the Rook and Bishop Mate.

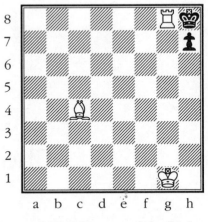

2nd Basic Pattern of the Rook and Bishop Mate.

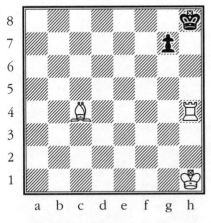

3rd Basic Pattern of the Rook and Bishop Mate.

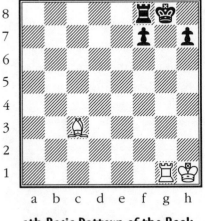

4th Basic Pattern of the Rook and Bishop Mate.

Rook and Bishop Mate Problems

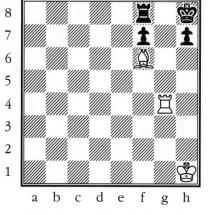

5th Basic Pattern of the Rook and Bishop Mate.

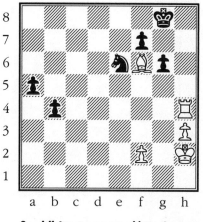

82. White to move. Mate in one.

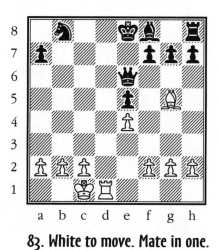

83. White to move. Mate in one.

84. Black to move. Mate in one.

Solutions:

82) 1. Rh8#

83) 1. Rd8#

84) 1. ...Ra3#

Rook and Bishop Mate Problems (continued)

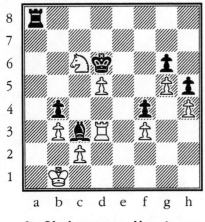

85. Black to move. Mate in one.

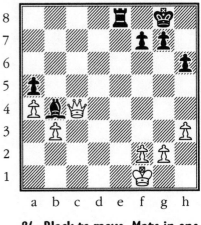

86. Black to move. Mate in one.

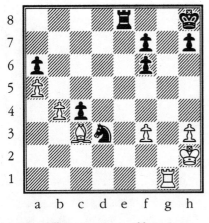

87. White to move. Mate in one.

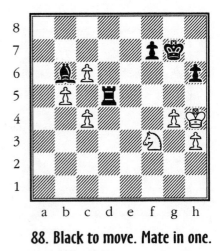

88. Black to move. Mate in one.

Solutions:
85) 1. ...Ra1#
86) 1. ...Re1#
87) 1. Bxf6#
88) 1. ...Bf2#

Rook and Bishop Mate Problems (continued)

89. White to move. Mate in one.

90. Black to move. Mate in one.

91. Black to move. Mate in one.

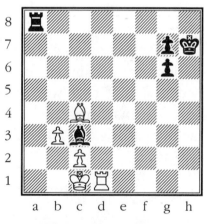

92. White to move. Mate in one.
Black to move. Mate in one.

Solutions:

89) 1. Ra8#
90) 1. ...Bh3#
91) 1. ...Bg2#
92) White: 1. Rh1#; Black 1. ...Ra1#

Rook and Knight Checkmates

One of the oldest checkmates in chess literature is the Arabian Mate, with a Knight and Rook. These two pieces, along with the King they have checkmated in the diagram below, are the only ones that still move the same way they did when chess was first invented over fourteen hundred years ago.

However, in addition to the Arabian Mate, there are many ways the Rook and Knight can work together to give checkmate. In some of our basic patterns there are other pieces helping out, either to guard one of the two major players (the Rook and Knight) or to help take away escape squares.

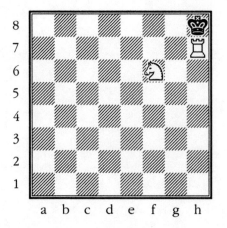

Rook and Knight Checkmate Patterns

1st Basic Pattern of the Rook and Knight Mate (Known as the Arabian Mate).

2nd Basic Pattern of the Rook and Knight Mate.

3rd Basic Pattern of the Rook and Knight Mate.

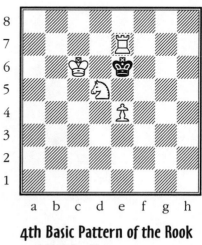

4th Basic Pattern of the Rook and Knight Mate.

Rook and Knight Checkmate Patterns (continued)

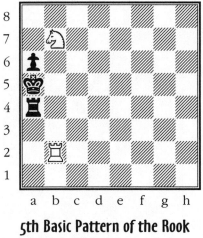

5th Basic Pattern of the Rook and Knight Mate.

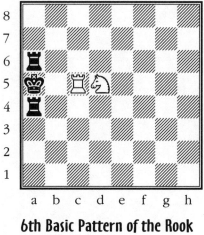

6th Basic Pattern of the Rook and Knight Mate.

Rook and Knight Checkmate Problems

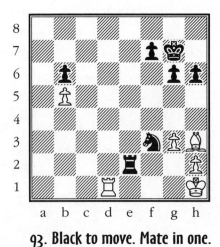

93. Black to move. Mate in one.

94. White to move. Mate in one.

Solutions:

93) 1. ...Rxh2#

94) 1. Rh3#

Rook and Knight Checkmate Problems (continued)

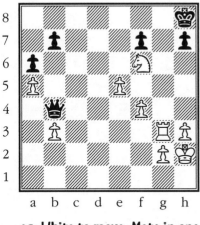

95. White to move. Mate in one.

96. White to move. Mate in one.

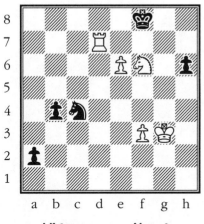

97. White to move. Mate in one.

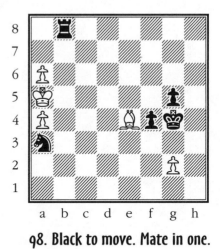

98. Black to move. Mate in one.

Solutions:
95) 1. Rg8#
96) 1. Ne7#
97) 1. Rf7#
98) 1. ...Nc4#

Rook and Knight Checkmate Problems (continued)

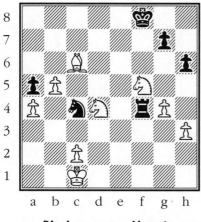

99. Black to move. Mate in one.

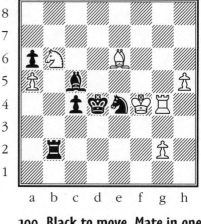

100. Black to move. Mate in one.

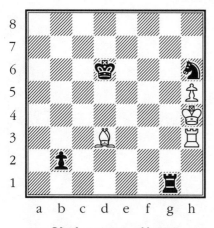

101. Black to move. Mate in one.

102. White to move. Mate in one.

Solutions:

99) 1. …Rf1#
100) 1. …Rf2#
101) 1. …Rg4#
102) 1. Nc2#

Bishop and Knight Checkmates

While the Bishop and Knight can certainly be major players in forcing checkmate, they always need a lot of help. The easiest place to checkmate a King is in the corner, where you only have to take away a block of four squares. Because of the peculiar limitations of the two minor pieces, they just can't do that alone. Quite often these two get a lot of assistance from the army of the King they are hunting, as in the diagram below.

Bishop and Knight Checkmate Patterns and Problems

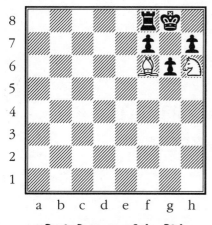

1st Basic Pattern of the Bishop and Knight Mate.

2nd Basic Pattern of the Bishop and Knight Mate.

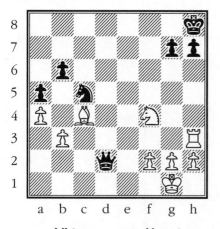

103. White to move. Mate in one.

104. Black to move. Mate in one.

Solutions:

103) 1. Ng6#
104) 1. ...Ne4#

Bishop and Knight Checkmate Problems

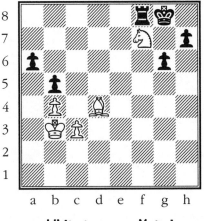

105. White to move. Mate in one.

106. Black to move. Mate in one.

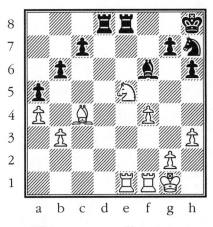

107. White to move. Mate in one.

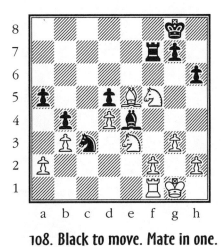

108. Black to move. Mate in one.

Solutions:

105) 1. Nh6#
106) 1. ...Be4#
107) 1. Ng6#
108) 1. ...Ne2#

chapter 17

Bishop Checkmates

As with the Bishop and Knight mates, the Bishop acting alone needs a lot of help, usually from its own army as well as some blocking assistance from the opposing forces. With a little help from their King, a pair of Bishops can force mate against a lone King (see puzzle #114).

Bishop Checkmate Patterns and Problems

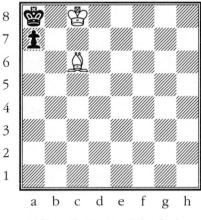

1st Basic Pattern of the Bishop Mate.

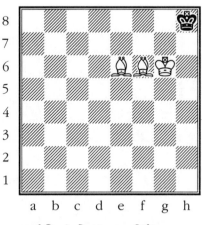

2nd Basic Pattern of the Bishop Mate.

109. Black to move. Mate in one.

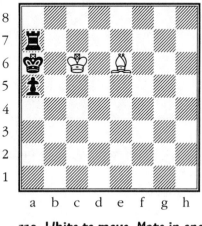

110. White to move. Mate in one.

Solutions:
109) 1. ...Bc3#
110) 1. Bc4#

Bishop Checkmate Problems

111. White to move. Mate in one.

112. White to move. Mate in one.

113. Black to move. Mate in one.

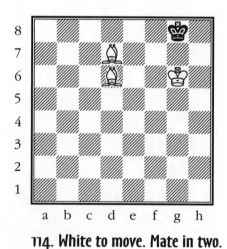

114. White to move. Mate in two.

Solutions:

111) 1. Bg6#
112) 1. Bf6#
113) 1. …Be8#
114) 1. Be6+, Kh8; 2. Be5#

c h a p t e r

18

Knight Checkmates

The Knight, like the Bishop, needs a lot of help to make a checkmate. The position below is often arrived at by way of a Queen sacrifice (see the Smothered Mate, Chapter 36).

A pair of Knights can sometimes team up in very surprising ways.

Knight Checkmate Patterns

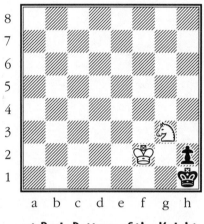

1st Basic Pattern of the Knight Mate.

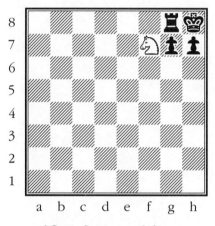

2nd Basic Pattern of the Knight Mate. Smothered Mate.

3rd Basic Pattern of the Knight Mate.

4th Basic Pattern of the Knight Mate.

Knight Checkmate Problems

115. Black to move. Mate in one.

116. Black to move. Mate in one.

117. Black to move. Mate in one.

118. Black to move. Mate in one.

Solutions:

115) 1. ...Nb6#
116) 1. ...Ne3#
117) 1. ...Nf2#
118) 1. ...Na5#

Knight Checkmate Problems (continued)

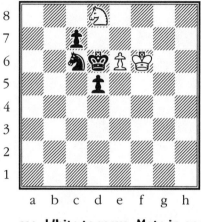

119. White to move. Mate in one.

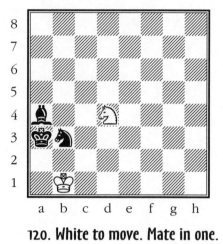

120. White to move. Mate in one.

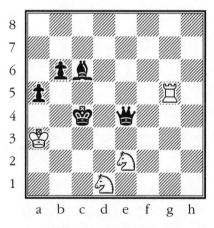

121. White to move. Mate in one.

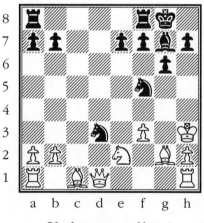

122. Black to move. Mate in one.

Solutions:
119) 1. Nb7#
120) 1. Nc2#
121) 1. Nb2#
122) 1. ...Nf2#

chapter 19

Pawn Checkmates

Every piece on the chessboard except the King can give a checkmate. Even the lowly Pawn can get in on the action, as the diagram below shows.

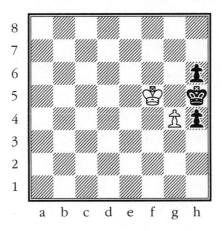

Pawn Checkmate Patterns

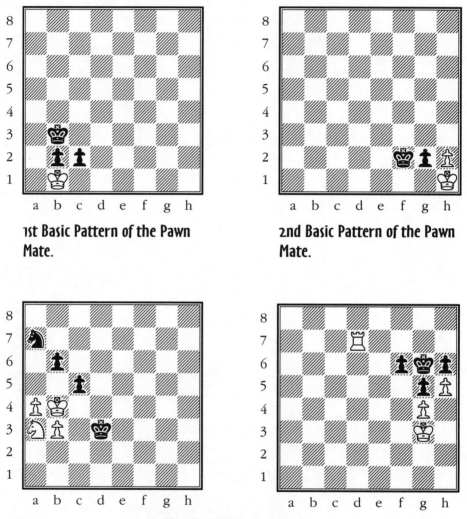

1st Basic Pattern of the Pawn Mate.

2nd Basic Pattern of the Pawn Mate.

Two More Pawn mates.

Pawn Checkmate Problems

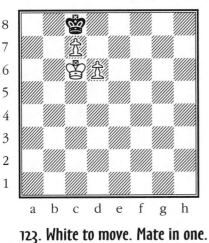

123. White to move. Mate in one.

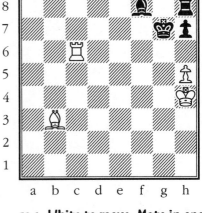

124. White to move. Mate in one.

125. Black to move. Mate in one.

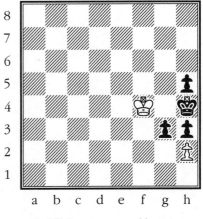

126. White to move. Mate in one.

Solutions:
123) 1. d7#
124) 1. h6#
125) 1. ...b2#
126) 1. hxg3#

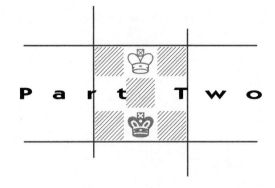

Part Two

Mixed Mate in One

In the next part we have forty diagrams of different types of checkmates in one move. Unlike the earlier checkmates, these are all mixed up, so you don't know ahead of time which pieces are needed to find a checkmate.

Some of them are fairly simple, others have little tricks in them, like a peculiar Knight move or a piece that looks as if could stop the mate but can't because it's pinned.

Look at the caption under the diagram carefully. Some, especially in the beginning, are a mate in one for both sides. In most, however, there is a mate only by White or only by Black.

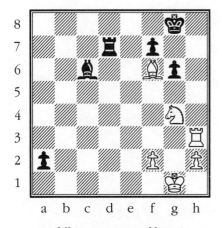

127. White to move. Mate in one.
Black to move. Mate in one.

128. White to move. Mate in one.
Black to move. Mate in one.

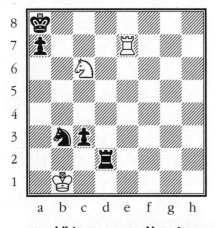

129. White to move. Mate in one.
Black to move. Mate in one.

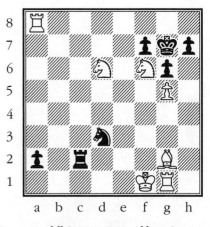

130. White to move. Mate in one.
Black to move. Mate in one.

Solutions:

127) White: 1. Rh8#; Black: 1. ...Rd1#
128) White: Ra2#; Black: 1. ...Rg1#
129) White: 1. Rxa7#; Black: 1. ...Rb2#
130) White: 1. Rg8#; Black: 1. ...Rf2#

Mixed Mate in One

131. White to move. Mate in one.
Black to move. Mate in one.

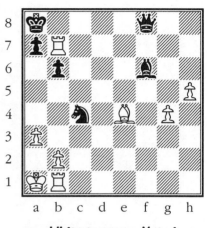

132. White to move. Mate in one.
Black to move. Mate in one.

133. White to move. Mate in one.
Black to move. Mate in one.

134. White to move. Mate in one.
Black to move. Mate in one.

Solutions:

131) White: 1. Nc2#; Black: 1. ...Bc3#
132) White: 1. Rxb6#; Black: 1. ...Qxa3#
133) White: 1. Bf5#; Black: 1. ...Qxh2#
134) White: 1. Ng6#; Black: 1. ...Ra1#

Mixed Mate in One (continued)

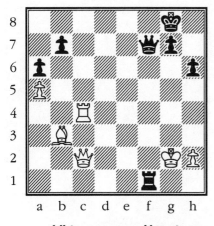

135. White to move. Mate in one.
Black to move. Mate in one.

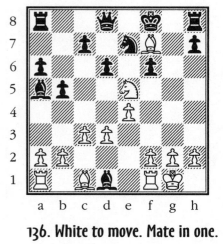

136. White to move. Mate in one.

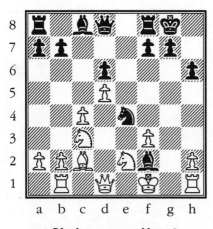

137. Black to move. Mate in one.

138. White to move. Mate in one.

Solutions:
135) White: 1. Rc8#; Black: 1. …Qf3#
136) 1. Bh6#
137) 1. …Bh3#
138) 1. Bd4#

Mixed Mate in One (continued)

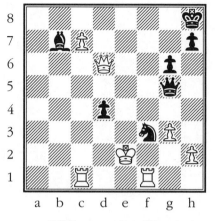

**139. White to move. Mate in one.
Black to move. Mate in one.**

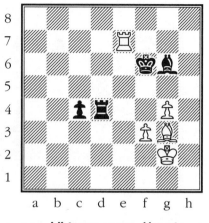

140. White to move. Mate in one.

**141. White to move. Mate in one.
Black to move. Mate in one.**

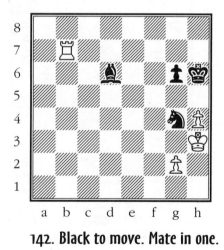

142. Black to move. Mate in one.

Solutions:
139) White: 1. Qf8#; Black: 1. ...Qd2#
140) 1. Bh4#
141) White: 1. Qxg7#; Black 1. ...Re1#
142) 1. ...Nf2#

Mixed Mate in One (continued)

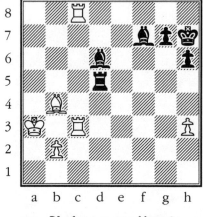

143. Black to move. Mate in one.

144. Black to move. Mate in one.

145. White to move. Mate in one.
Black to move. Mate in one.

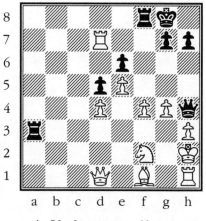

146. Black to move. Mate in one.

Solutions:

143) 1. ...Ra5#
144) 1. ...Qxf2#
145) White: 1. Bf5#; Black: 1. ...Qg2#
146) 1. ...Qg3#

Mixed Mate in One (continued)

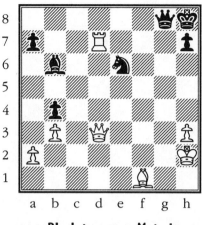

147. Black to move. Mate in one.

148. Black to move. Mate in one.

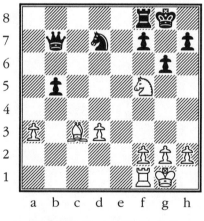

149. White to move. Mate in one.

150. White to move. Mate in one.

Solutions:

147) 1. ...Qg1#
148) 1. ...Qd3#
149) 1. Nh6# or Ne7#
150) 1. Rh3#

Mixed Mate in One (continued)

151. White to move. Mate in one.

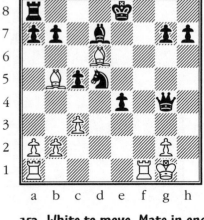

152. White to move. Mate in one.

153. Black to move. Mate in one.

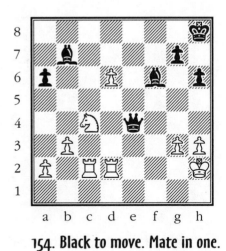

154. Black to move. Mate in one.

Solutions:

151) 1. Rh5#
152) 1. Rf8#
153) 1. ...Rh5#
154) 1. ...Qh1#

Mixed Mate in One (continued)

155. Black to move. Mate in one.

156. Black to move. Mate in one.

157. White to move. Mate in one.

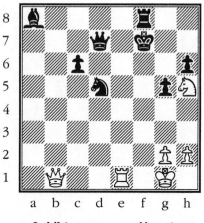

158. White to move. Mate in one.

Solutions:
155) 1. ...Nf4#
156) 1. ...Rh1#
157) 1. Bf6#
158) 1. Qh7#

Mixed Mate in One (continued)

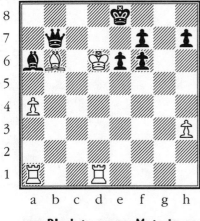

159. Black to move. Mate in one.

160. White to move. Mate in one.

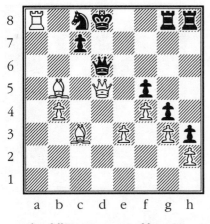

161. White to move. Mate in one.

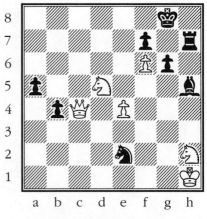

**162. White to move. Mate in one.
Black to move. Mate in one.**

Solutions:

159) 1. ...Qxb6#

160) 1. c3#

161) 1. Bf6#

162) White: 1. Qc8#; Black: 1. ...Bf3#

Mixed Mate in One (continued)

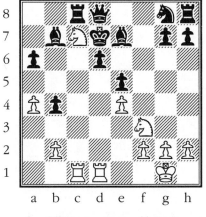

163. White to move. Mate in one.

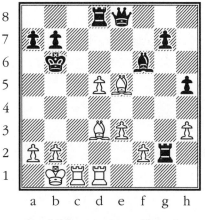

164. White to move. Mate in one.

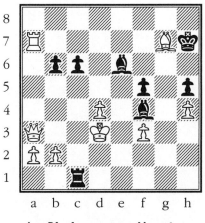

165. Black to move. Mate in one.

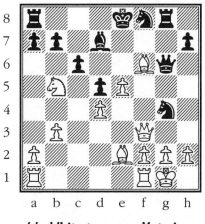

166. White to move. Mate in one.

Solutions:

163) 1. Nxe5#
164) 1. Bc7#
165) 1. ...Bc4#
166) 1. Nd6#

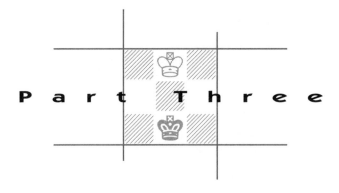

More Mating Patterns

Except for the mate with the King and Queen and the mate with the King and Rook, most of the patterns we have shown to this point have been simple one-move ideas. We now move to patterns that are more complex, requiring several moves to implement. You may recognize some of the final positions from our earlier patterns.

In a few of the mating patterns, for example the two Lolli mates, there are alternative checkmates that can be found, but the purpose here is to demonstrate the main pattern.

Notation:

Also, in an effort to show the **long form algebraic notation**, all notation in this and the next section is long form algebraic.

c h a p t e r

21

The Blind Swine Checkmate

The checkmate that follows from the position in this diagram is called the Blind Swine Mate. Perhaps the name comes from the fact that we call a Rook on the seventh rank a pig (because there are usually a lot of enemy Pawns for the Rook to root around in, or maybe it's because a Rook on the seventh hogs the board), and with doubled Rooks on the seventh rank, even a couple of blind pigs could find this checkmate. Actually, this pattern got its name from David Janowski (1868–1927), a Polish Grandmaster who referred to a pair of Rooks on the seventh rank that could not find a mate as "blind swine." In this pattern, they do find the mate, so maybe we should change the name, but somehow "the sighted swine checkmate" doesn't sound right.

The Rook battery on the seventh rank is a powerful weapon. First the Rook on e7 removes the King's Pawn cover with a pair of checks, then the second Rook on b7 comes in to deliver the final blow.

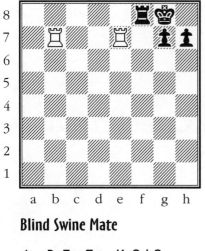

Blind Swine Mate

Final position for the Blind Swine Mate.

1. Re7xg7+ Kg8-h8
2. Rg7xh7+ Kh8-g8
3. Rb7-g7#

In this position, Paul Morphy (see Chapter 23) found a way to force the Blind Swine Mate.

1. Rd7-g7+ Kg8-h8
2. Nh7-f8! threatening 3. Nf8-g6#, thereby forcing Black to capture, which fences in the Black King perfectly for the Blind Swine Mate.

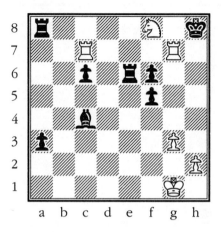

2. ...   Ra8xf8 Now Morphy has the Black King right where he wants it: blocked in with just two squares to move on. With two White Rooks to cover both squares, the Black King is not long for this game.

3. Rg7-h7+   Kh8-g8

4. Rc7-g7#

Anastasia's Mate

This checkmate gets its name not from a real chess player, but from a fictional character in a German novel published in 1803.

There are many ways to arrive at the final mating position, but the essential idea is that the enemy King is pushed around on the edge of the board by a Knight check, and then a sacrifice opens a line of attack for a Rook or Queen to inflict a variation of the corridor mate on the poor monarch.

In this position, for example, a Knight check on e7 chases the King into the corner. Then a Queen sacrifice on h7 pulls the King up the h-file, where it is imprisoned by the Knight attack on g8 and g6 and its own Pawn on g7. That's a perfect set-up for a variation of the corridor mate.

Anastasia's Mate

1. Nd5-e7+ Kg8-h8
2. Qe4xh7+ Kh8xh7
3. Rc5-h5#

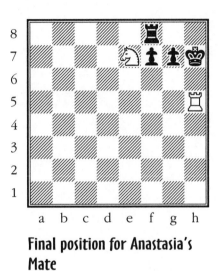

Final position for Anastasia's Mate

Morphy's Mate

Paul Morphy was one of the greatest geniuses ever to play chess. Born in New Orleans in 1837, he showed his talent for chess in early childhood. By the time he was twenty-one, he completely dominated the chess world. Morphy was one of the first to grasp the power of rapid development and the importance of King safety in the opening. He also appreciated the value of open lines for an attack in the middlegame, sacrificing whenever necessary to force his attack to completion. In this checkmate, he is even willing to sacrifice his Queen to get his attack rolling. Naturally, you don't want to go around giving up your Queen senselessly, but in this case, Morphy has a clear vision of how the opposing King's head will be his reward.

First the Queen removes the Black Bishop on f6, setting up a mating battery with the Bishop, aimed at g7. That forces Black to take the Queen with the g-Pawn, which has the terrible result of the opening of the g-file for a Rook check on g1. The King has only one place to hide: h8. Unfortunately, h8 is on the same diagonal as the Bishop on c3, with only the unguarded Pawn on f6 between.

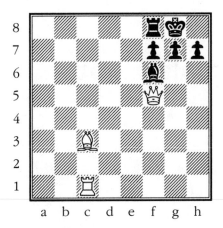

Morphy's Mate

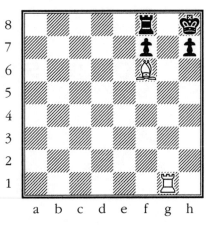

Final position for Morphy's Mate.

1. Qf5xf6   g7xf6
2. Rc1-g1 +   Kg8-h8
3. Bc3xf6 #

Morphy's Concealed Mate

This one takes a couple of more moves than the previous position, but then we don't have to give up the Queen this time either.

In this checkmate, we only sacrifice our opponent's pieces. The opportunity to open the g-file is still there, because the Bishop and Rook converge on g7. When the Rook picks off the g7 Pawn, the King has to hide in the corner, where it can do nothing to protect itself from a discovered check when the Rook moves away. A mistake would be to pull the Rook back immediately, because Black can block the discovered check with the f7-Pawn. Another mistake many beginners make is to rush down with the Rook to g8 with a double check. The Black King simply escapes both checks by taking the Rook for free. Instead, White should take off the f7-Pawn with a discovered check. Then, when the Black King returns to g8, go back for another check with the Rook on

g7. This time when the Black King escapes to h8, the Rook can pull back along the g-file with a discovered check and the f-Pawn can't block the check; it's off the board. Instead, Black has to block with the Rook from f8 to f6. However, since the Rook is unguarded, the Bishop simply swoops down to take it for a checkmate.

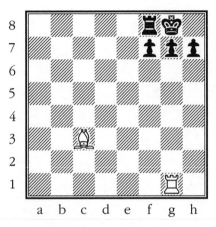

Morphy's Concealed Mate

1. Rg1xg7+   Kg8-h8
2. Rg7xf7dis+* Kh8-g8
3. Rf7-g7+   Kg8-h8
4. Rg7-g5dis+   Rf8-f6
5. Bc6xf6#

*Not 2. Rg7-g5dis+?, f7-f6!
The key to this is to eliminate
the f-Pawn.

Final position for Morphy's Concealed Mate.

c h a p t e r

25

Pillsbury's Mate

Harry Nelson Pillsbury was another great American chess wizard. Born in 1872, he didn't learn to play chess until he was sixteen, but in just five years he had established himself as one of the strongest players in the world by winning the prestigious tournament at Hastings, England in 1895 ahead of Lasker and Steinitz. Lasker had won the world championship the year before by beating Steinitz, who had been the world champion. Pillsbury was also an exceptional blindfold chess player, able to take on twenty opponents without looking at the boards.

The Pillsbury mate is similar to the Morphy Mate, but this time we have an extra Rook in reserve to make the mate happen a little faster. Here we also see the power of a double check.

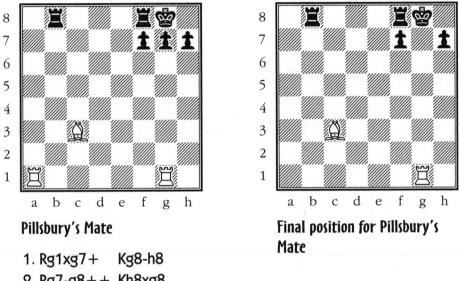

Pillsbury's Mate

Final position for Pillsbury's Mate

1. Rg1xg7+   Kg8-h8
2. Rg7-g8++   Kh8xg8
3. Ra1-g1#

The double check on move two forces the King to capture the Rook. Taking with the Rook on f8 still leaves the Bishop check in force, and blocking the Bishop check still leaves the Rook check. The only escape from a double check is that the King must move. In this case, it has to move and capture the White Rook on g8.

Lolli's Mate

Giambattista Lolli (1698–1769) was the oldest of three great players—del Rio and Ponziani were the others—who must have had great fun playing chess together in the town of Modena, Italy. In this book we have two checkmates that were attributed to Lolli.

In the first, the Pawn on f6, attacking g7, provides the threat that induces all the moves in this mate. White threatens to give checkmate on g7 by slithering the powerful Queen over to h6. Black has just enough time to guard against that attack. However, White has another trick in mind, based on the Rook lurking in the corner on a1. A shocking Queen sacrifice brings the attack home.

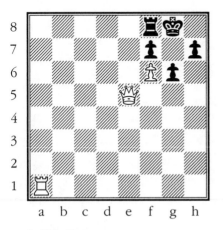

Lolli's Mate

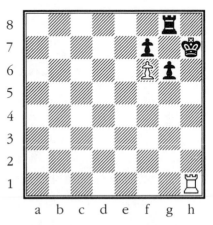

Final position for Lolli's Mate

1.	Qe5-g5	Kg8-h8
2.	Qg5-h6	Rf8-g8

Black breathes a sigh of relief. He thinks he's safe.

   3.   Qh6xh7+! Uh oh. What's this?

3.	...	Kxh7
4.	Ra1-h1#	

Lolli's Mate II

In this variation of Lolli's Mate the Pawn on f6 again provides the threat of mate on g7. However, there is also another threat: Ne5xf7. At present, both moves are suicide since, if the Knight jumps down to f7, the Queen on a7 can simply capture it, and the Rook on g8 prevents the White Queen from getting safely to g7. Lolli's solution is a marvelous deflection. It puts stress on either the Black Rook on g8 or the Black Queen on a7. We start with **1. Rb5-b8!**

Lolli's Mate

Final position for Lolli's Mate

1. Rb5-b8!   Qa7xb8
2. Ne5xf7#

or

1. Rb5-b8!   Rg8xb8
2. Qh6-g7#

28

Blackburne's Mate

Joseph Henry Blackburne (1841–1924) was one of the greatest players of his day. He met all the top players of the last part of the nineteenth and the early twentieth centuries in tournaments throughout Europe. Nicknamed "The Black Death," he found many devastating Kingside attacks in his long career.

The mate given below is a perfect example of his multi-pronged attacks. With four pieces aimed at the weakened Black Kingside, something has to give.

The first shot, 1. Qxh5, threatens two different mates: 2. Qh7#, supported by the Knight on g5, and 2. Qh8#, protected by the Bishop on b2. Taking the Queen is forced, but that only opens the door to another mate.

Blackburne's Mate

1. Qd1xh5   g6xh5
2. Bd3-h7#

Final position for Blackburne's Mate

29

Blackburne's Mate II

In the previous mate by Blackburne, he had several pieces bearing down on the opposing King, and he found several ways to win. Such a grand display of force leaves the other side helpless. He can do no more than choose which mate to fall victim to.

Here again, the marvelous Blackburne simply overpowers his foe. 1. Qh6 threatens mate on g7, with three pieces converging on that square. Taking the Knight stops nothing, since the Bishop also hits g7 allowing Qxg7#. Taking the Queen doesn't even work, since that walks right into a pretty Bishop and Knight mate.

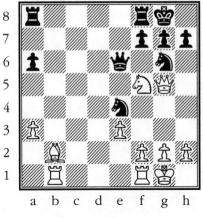

Blackburne's Mate II

Final Position for Blackburne's Mate II

1. Qg5-h6   g7xh6
2. Nf5xh6#

Anderssen's Mate

Adolph Anderssen (1818–1879) was a brilliant attacking player, his reputation firmly established by, among many other achievements, being on the winning side of what have been dubbed "The Immortal Game" and "The Evergreen Game."

In what has come to be known as Anderssen's Mate, there is a close relation to Blackburne's mate. In both, the pair of Bishops raking the weakened Kingside prove too much to withstand.

Notice that 1. Qe2-h5, preparing a mate on h7, won't work. Not only can Black just block the Bishop's protection of h7 by playing 1. ... f7-f5, but, far worse, with the Black Queen and Bishop battery aimed at the White Rook on f2, and the further problem of the Black Bishop on b7 aiming at g2, it is Black who would win with a mate in two. Don't prepare to do what you can do immediately.

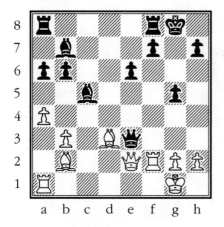

Anderssen's Mate

1. Bd3xh7+ Kg8xh7
2. Qe2-h5+ Kh7-g8
3. Qh5-h8#

Final positon for Anderssen's Mate

Greco's Mate

Gioacchino Greco (1600-1634) was born into poverty, but in his short life became one of the strongest players of the seventeenth century. Playing in his native Italy, and then traveling to France, England, and Spain, he took on all comers and was honored at the court of Phillip IV. He wrote many manuscripts, dedicated to his various patrons, that were translated into English, French, Dutch, German, and Danish.

Greco's Mate features an elegant bit of maneuvering to force an attractive Queen and Bishop mate. First, Greco chases the King to the corner. Then, there is a Knight and Queen mate threat. When Black stops the threat by a Pawn advance and then a Pawn capture of the White Knight, the White Queen simply backs up for the kill.

Greco's Mate

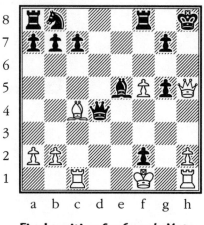

Final position for Greco's Mate

1. Bd3-c4+ Kg8-h8
2. Ne4-g5 h7-h6
3. Qh5-g6 h6xNg5
4. Qg6-h5#

Damiano's Mate

Pedro Damiano, (died in 1544) was a Portuguese apothecary who wrote the first book of chess published in Italy. He also has the dubious distinction of having an opening that he analyzed as horrible named after him (1. e4, e5; 2. Nf3, f6? Damiano knew this was awful, but somehow his name got attached to it). His book has some rather excellent advice that teachers still tell their students to this day. One example is, "when you see a good move, look for a better one." Keep that one in mind when you play.

In this mating pattern, a Pawn on g6 keeps the Black King down. A double Rook sacrifice brings the Queen into play for mate.

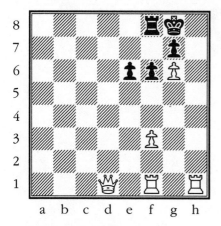

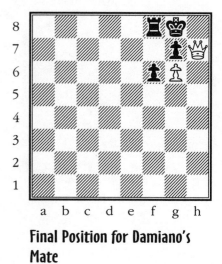

Damiano's Mate

Final Position for Damiano's Mate

1. Rh1-h8+   Kg8xh8
2. Rf1-h1+   Kh8-g8
3. Rh1-h8+   Kg8xh8
4. Qd1-h1+   Kh8-g8
5. Qh1-h7#

Boris Spassky, the World Champion from 1967 to 1972, found a way to force Damiano's mate in this position. Knowing the past prepares you for the future.

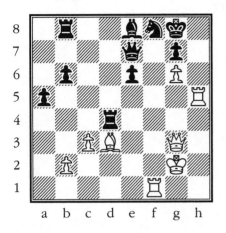

1. **Rf1xf8+   Qe7xf8**

Forced. If the King recaptures, the other White Rook mates on h8.

This capture by the Queen also stops the convergence of the Black Queen and Rook on h4, which would mess up the White Queen's aim down the h-file.

2. **Rh5-h8+   Kg8xh8**

3. **Qg3-h3+** and there is no way to stop the Queen mate on h7.

Damiano's Mate II

Naturally enough, in his book Damiano discussed more than one mating pattern. The one on the previous page with the double Rook sacrifice was emphasized by Vukovic in his excellent book *The Art of Attack in Chess*. Koltanowski and Finkelstein in another great book, *Checkmate!*, mention this second Damiano pattern.

Although there are four other possible first moves for a mate in two, Damiano's idea was to play 1. Qa5xa6+ forcing the King to b8 where the Queen, supported by the Bishop, would deliver mate on the focal point b7. 1. Qb6, 1. Qb4, 1. Qc7, and 1. Qd5 also force a mate in two.

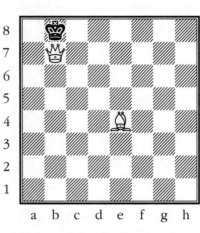

Damiano's Mate II

1. Qa5xa6+ Ka8-b8
2. Qa6xb7#

Final position for Damiano's Mate II

Damiano's Mate III

On the previous page, we mentioned two excellent books that refer to two different patterns associated with Damiano. In a third book, *The Art of Checkmate*, by Renaud and Kahn, the authors give a third pattern related to the Damiano mate. It is very useful to know this pattern.

In this pattern, the winning side has control over the two squares diagonally on either side in front of the weak King. In the diagram below these are h7 and f7, covered by the Pawn on g6. If the strong player's Queen can get to one of those squares, it will force the King under the other one. When the Queen slides over to the other one, the result will be a very nice checkmate.

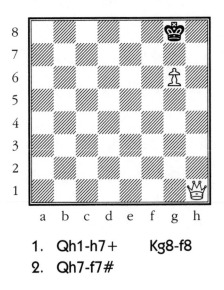

1. Qh1-h7+   Kg8-f8
2. Qh7-f7#

Final position for Damiano Mate III

The Third Damiano Mate in Practice

In this position, White saw a chance to get the previous checkmate pattern. He has the required protection over the two squares diagonally up from the enemy King. The problem is that Bishop in the middle. How can White force Black to move the Bishop out of the way?

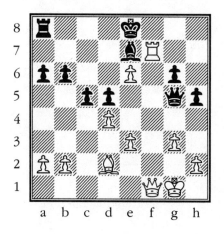

The answer is a Rook sacrifice.

   1. Rf7-f8+ Be7xf8 (the only move)

Now the way is clear.

   2. Qf1-f7+ Ke8-d8 Right under the focal point d7.

   3. Qf7-d7#

Damiano's Third Mate with a Queen and Bishop

The mating pattern in this position is directly related to the previous pattern. This time we set it up with a Bishop Sacrifice. Then the Queen and the remaining Bishop do a little dance with the enemy King, swirling him from side to side until he can't stand any longer.

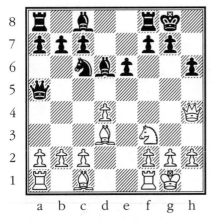

Bishop Sacrifice on h6

1. Bc1xh6	g7xh6
2. Qh4xh6	Rf8-e8 to

give the King running room.
(If black tries,

2. …	f7-f5, then
3. Qh6-g6+	Kg8-h8
4. Nf3-g5 with an unstoppable mate next move.)	

In this position, many people are tempted to go astray. The immediate and appealing Queen check on h7 doesn't quite work. The King can slip away via f8 and e7.

3. Bd3-h7+! Go in with the Bishop first! The Queen stops the King's escape to f8 and forces the King into the corner. Now we have a neat little discovered check, followed by our mate in two pattern.

3. …	Kg8-h8
4. Bh7-g6 dis+	Kh8-g8
5. Qh6-h7+	Kg8-f8
6. Qh7-f7#	

35

Mate with a Queen and Knight

This is an interesting pattern. It's easy to miss because it looks so much like a simple support mate on h7. However, since it is **Black to move**, that pattern disappears on the first move.

Black to move.

Here the only way to escape mate is to get the Rook out of the way so the King can run from the coming check on h7. So,

1. ...   **Rf8-b8** but now White doesn't go for the check on h7. Instead,

2. **Qh5xf7+!**   **Kg8-h8** and now the Knight swings over to make g7 a focal point for mate.

3. **Ng5-e6!**   **Rb8-g8** the most likely way to stop mate on g7, but now,

4. **Qf7-h5#!**

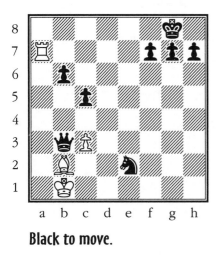

Black to move.

In this position, Black found a quick mate—and a good thing too, since White has a mate in one on the back rank.

1. ...   Ne2xc3+
2. Kb1-a1 (If 2. Ka1-c1, then
2. ...Qb3-d1# is very pretty)
2. ...   Qb3-d1+
3. Bb2-c1 (the only move)
3. ...   Qd1xc1#

Mate with a Queen and Knight

This is another neat pattern, based on the Knight posting itself on f5. Often a Knight on f5 can cause serious problems in the Black camp.

Recognizing this, Black is about to remove the knight with the d7-Bishop. The Pawn protecting the Knight is pinned to the White Queen, so this would be a free piece. White makes an exchange sacrifice, eliminating the Bishop, and then sweeps the Queen out for a dangerous pair of threats.

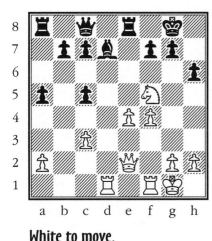

White to move.

1. Rd1xd7 Qc8xd7
2. Qe2-g4! threatening both
3. Qg4xg7# and
3. Nf5-h6+ with a discovery on the unguarded Black Queen.

White wins because Black cannot possibly meet both threats. Either the Queen or the King goes next move.

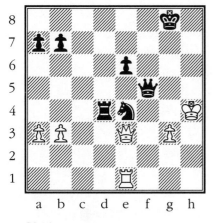

Black to move.

We close this chapter with a clever maneuver by Tal.

1. ...   Ne4-d2 dis+!
2. Qe3xd4   Nd2-f3#

Smothered Mate

The Smothered Mate, involving a Queen sacrifice and a mate by the lone Knight, is one of the most elegant demonstrations of the power of a good position over a material advantage. It is also one of the most surprising mates in chess.

First, the Queen gives a check that forces the King to the corner. If it runs to f8, then Qf7# stops the game right there. After the King hides in the corner, the Knight hops down to f7+ to chase it back out. When the King makes its only move, stepping over to g8 again, the Knight makes the key move, leaping over to h6 for a double check. Again the King has to hide in the corner, since moving to f8 still allows the Queen to mate on f7. Then the White Queen surprises the Black King with her cozy check on g8. The Black King cannot take, as the White Queen is protected by the White Knight on h6. This forces the Black Rook to capture, but now the King has no breathing room. The Knight returns to f7 for a neat smothered mate.

Smothered Mate

Final position for the Smothered Mate

1.	Qd4-d5+	Kg8-h8*
2.	Ng5-f7+	Kh8-g8
3.	Nf7-h6++	Kg8-h8*
4.	Qd5-g8+	Re8xg8
5.	Nh6-f7#	

*if ... Kg8-f8, then 2.Qd5-f7#

Smothered Mate in the Opening

Surprisingly, there is a way to play for the smothered mate right in the beginning of the game. This one is worth knowing, if only to keep from falling for it.

After the opening moves:

1. e2-e4   e7-e5
2. Ng1-f3   Nb8-c6
3. Bf1-c4   Nc6-d4

Many young players can't resist taking the Pawn on e5 and threatening a Knight fork on f7, hitting the Black Queen on d8 and the Black Rook on h8. So,

4. Nf3xe5

Now comes a little surprise:

4. ...   Qd8-g5

The Knight fork is still on, and it's too much to resist.

5. Ne5xf7   Qg5xg2 **Bigger surprise.**

Uh oh. Have to save the Rook on h1. No matter, the Rook on h8 is still trapped.

6. Rh1-f1   Qg2xe4+!

Oops. Didn't see that one either. Hmm. Can't guard with the Queen, since the pesky Knight on d4 could take her. Have to block with the Bishop, even though that will leave the Knight on f7 unguarded…

7. Bc4-e2   Nd4-f3#!!

Oh, my. Have to remember this one!

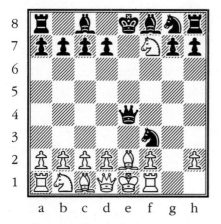

Final position for the Smothered Mate in the Opening

White can avoid this debacle by simply taking the Knight on the fourth move.

Another Smothered Mate

In the position below, Jose Raul Capablanca, the third World Champion (1921–27), found a three move smothered mate.

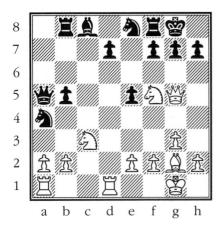

Black has four pieces away from the action on the Kingside. Allowing a Queen and Knight to roam unchallenged and near the King is an invitation to disaster.

The Knight on e8 seems to be holding out against the threatened mate on g7. However, now Capablanca shifts the attack.

    1. **Nf5-h6+** **Kg8-h8** (the only move)

    2. **Qg5-e7!** Threatens mate by capturing the Rook on f8 (Next Diagram).

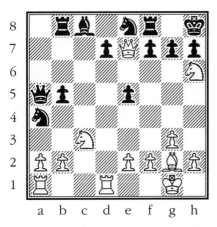

Black has no choice. The Rook must move to g8.

    2. ...   Rf8-g8

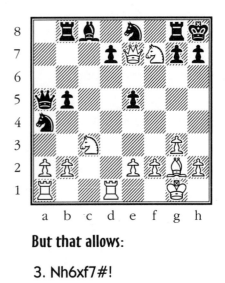

But that allows:

    3. Nh6xf7#!

Boden's Mate *or* the Criss-Cross Mate

Boden's Mate is often set up with an initial Queen sacrifice, as in the diagram below.

The key features of this mating pattern are:

1. The King is hemmed in on one side, either by his own pieces (frequently a Rook and Knight as in this diagram), or by an enemy Rook attacking down the open file;

2. The King is blocked from moving forward or to the side by a slashing enemy Bishop;

3. The second enemy Bishop delivers checkmate along the exposed diagonal leading to the King.

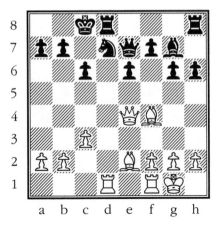

1. Qe4xc6+!

Black has no choice on this move:

1. ...   b7xc6

And now the diagonal is open for

2. Be2-a6#.

This is a typical Boden's Mate position. The King is hemmed in on the d-file, the White Bishop on f4 restricts his forward and sideways movement, and the only protection on the a6-c8 diagonal is the Pawn on b7, which also happens to be the sole support of the Pawn on c6. White opens the diagonal with a Queen sacrifice.

Boden's Mate

167. Black to move. Mate in two.

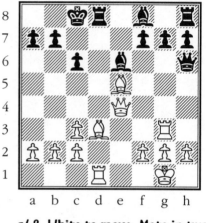

168. White to move. Mate in two.

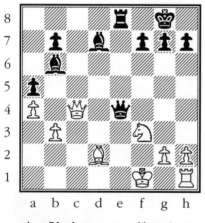

169. Black to move. Mate in two.

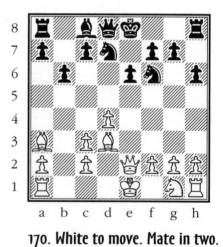

170. White to move. Mate in two.

Solutions:

167) 1. ...Qc3+; 2. bxc3, Ba3#
168) 1. Qxc6+, bxc6; 2. Ba6#
169) 1. ...Qxf3+; 2. gxf3, Bh3#
170) 1. Qxe6+, fxe6; 2. Bg6#

c h a p t e r

38

Legal's Mate

De Legal (1702–1792), the teacher of the great Philidor, was one of the strongest players in France in the mid-1700s. His game with St. Brie, given below, shows the earliest recorded version of a Queen sacrifice followed by mate with the minor pieces in the opening.

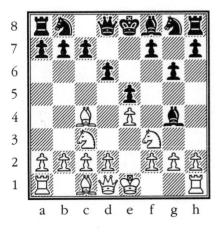

1.	e2-e4	e7-e5
2.	Ng1-f3	d7-d6
3.	Bf1-c4	Bc8-g4

Not a good move. This premature pin is useless. Better would be to get out a Knight.

4. Nb1-c3   g7-g6?

Two weak moves in the opening are more than Black can afford.

Now Legal has a little fun with his less experienced opponent.

171

5. Nf3xe5! St. Brie was no doubt very happy to take off the master's Queen here.

5. ...   Bg4xd1

However, he should have been content to play 5. ...dxe5 and be down a Pawn after 6. Qxg4.

6. Bc4xf7+   Ke8-e7

7. Nc3-d5#

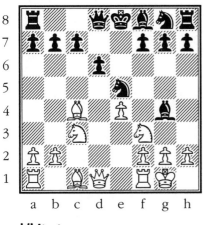

White to move.

Here again we have a position ripe for the Legal offer of a Queen to force a minor piece mate. Black has just foolishly piled on the pinned Knight at f3 with Nc6-e5, not realizing the danger in the position. Now comes the surprise:

1. Nf3xe5   Bg4xd1?
2. Bc4xf7+   Ke8-e7
3. Nc3-d5#

Black to move.

Black springs the surprise in this slightly more subtle version of the Legal Mate,.

1. ...   Nf6xe4
2. Bg5xe7?   Bc5xf2+
3. Ke1-f1   Ne4-g3#

c h a p t e r

39

Mate in Two/Mate in Three

171. Black to move. Mate in two.

172. Black to move. Mate in two.

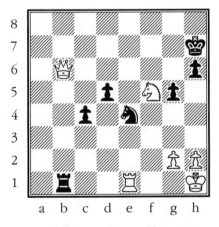

173. White to move. Mate in two.
Black to move. Mate in two.

174. Black to move. Mate in two.

Solutions:

171) 1. ...Qe1; 2. Bf1, Qxf1#

172) 1. ...Rh1+; 2. Kxh1, Qxf1#

173) White: 1. Qxh6+, Kg8; 2. Qg7#; Black: 1. ...Rxe1+; 2. Qg1, Nf2#

174) 1. ...Qxc3+; 2. bxc3, Ba3#

Mate in Two/Mate in Three

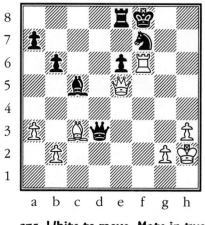

175. White to move. Mate in two.

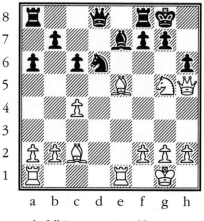

176. White to move. Mate in two.

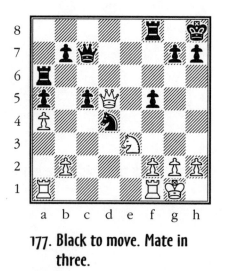

177. Black to move. Mate in three.

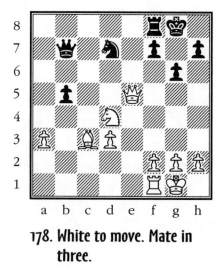

178. White to move. Mate in three.

Solutions:
175) 1. Rxf7+, Kxf7; 2. Qg7# or 1. ...Kg8; 2. Qg7#
176) 1. Qxh6, threatening mate on h7 or g7, forcing 1. ...gxh6; 2. Bh7#
177) 1. ...Ne2+; 2. Kh1, Qxh2+; 3. Kxh2, Rh6#
178) 1. Qg7+, Kxg7; 2. Nf5++, Kg8; 3. Nh6# or Ne7#

Part Four

c h a p t e r

40

Mating Attacks

In this section we are going to examine some much trickier positions than we have seen up to this point. We'll begin at an easy level, then climb quickly to the stars.

It isn't often that your opponents will just walk into a mate in one. Most of the time you will have to prepare the position so you can get the checkmate. The first step is to recognize what checkmate looks like. By the time you are reading this, you should have a good grasp of the fundamentals of checkmate. The positions in Part III were intended to provide some interesting new ideas. This section is designed to further expand your understanding of checkmate.

Nearly all the positions in this section are taken from master play, and demonstrate how deeply into a position the great players look.

Good chess players study the great masters of the past and present. In seeing how others have solved certain problems on the chessboard, we learn new tricks and ideas that we can implement in our own games.

One of the great chess teachers of the twentieth century, Jack Collins, recommended that young players study one hundred games of each of the World Champions. Among those directly influenced by Jack Collins were Bobby Fischer, Donald and Robert Byrne, and William Lomardy. Jack was on to an important truth: *studying the great ideas of others improves your own thoughts.*

The positions given in this section could be multiplied ten thousand times and still not exhaust the subject; but this is a good place to start.

You will notice in the examples in this section that there are a lot of tactical tricks used to set up the checkmate. The more deeply you study tactics—pins, forks, skewers, discoveries, decoys, deflections, removing the guard, and others—the more easily you will be able to get to the checkmates we've been studying in this book. You will also find that the final positions are much like the mate in one puzzles from Part One and Part Two of this book, and that the methods of achieving the mates are often related to the longer mating patterns of Part Three.

And now it's time to enjoy the work of the masters as they launch their mating attacks.

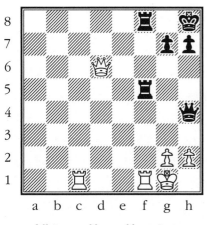

1. White to Move. Mate in two.

The Back Rank Mate often has to be set up with tactical shots. Our first position is a fairly simple example featuring a Queen attack with X-ray protection from the Rook on f1.

1. Qd6xf8+   Rf5xf8
2. Rf1xf8#

The second diagram shows a Queen sacrifice forcing an *absolute pin* to secure the checkmate.

1. Qf3xf7+   Rf8xf7
2. Re1-e8#

The White Bishop on b3 pins the Black Rook to the King.

2. White to Move. Mate in two.

Mating Attacks

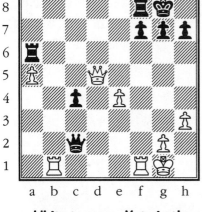

3. White to move. Mate in three.

This time we have another Queen sacrifice to deflect the f8-Rook from the back rank, and from then on it's simple brute force: White will get more attackers on f8 than Black has defenders.

   1.   **Qd5xf7+**   **Rf8xf7** if 1. ... Kg8-h8; 2. Qf7xf8#
   2.   **Rb1-b8+**   **Rf7-f8** the only move.
   3.   **R** (either)**xf8#**

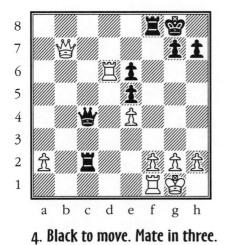

4. Black to move. Mate in three.

This position features exactly the same theme as the one above, but the moves are quite different.

   1.   ...   **Rc2xf2** threatening mate on f1.
   2.   **Rf1xf2**   **Qc4-c1+**
   3.   **Rf2-f1**   **Qc1xf1#** or
   3.   ...   **Rf8xf1#**

White could have delayed this with a couple of suicide checks (2. Qb7xg7+, Kg8xg7 and 3. Rd6-d7+), but that wouldn't change the result. Black still gets the win.

Mating Attacks

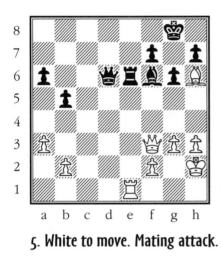

5. **White to move. Mating attack.**

This time the Queen sacrifice threatens mate in one with the Queen, and taking the Queen allows a pretty Bishop and Rook mate.

    1. **Qf3xf6** threatens mate in one on g7.

    1. ...   **Re6xg6** stops the mate on g7, but it also opens the e-file for a neat Bishop and Rook mate.

    2. **Re1-e8+ Qd6-f8**

    3. **Re8xf8#**

As in the previous diagram, there is a way for Black to delay the outcome with a desperado check (1. ...Qe6xg3+), but Black is still hopelessly lost.

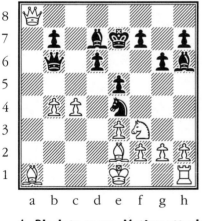

6. **Black to move. Mating attack.**

Although White appears to have a lot of pieces near the King, they are not well placed for defense; the Knight and Bishops don't hit the same squares, and the White King is dangerously exposed. Black comes crashing through with an unstoppable series of mating threats.

1.	...	Qb6xb4+
2.	Ke1-f1	Qb5-b1+
3.	Nf3-e1	Ne4-d2+
4.	Kf1-g1	Qb1xe1+
5.	Be2-f1	Qe1xf1#

If White had played 2. Ke1-d1, then 2. ...Qb4-b1#.

If White blocks the first check with 2. Nf3-d2, then 2. ...Qb4xd2+; 3. Ke1-f1, Qd2-c1+; 4. Be2-d1, Qc1xd1#.

If White blocks the first check with 2. Ba1-c3, Qb4xc3+ and Black is back in business as before, just delayed by one move.

Mating Attacks

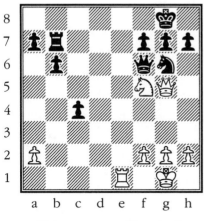

7. White to move. Mate in four.

This dazzling attack by Alekhine features two deflections and a decoy to set up a lone piece checkmate by the White Queen.

1. Re1-e8+ deflecting the Black Knight.

1. ... Ng6-f8

2. Nf5-h6+ Deflecting the Queen from the d8-h4 diagonal.

2. ... Qf6xh6 (2. ...Kg8-h8 allows 3. Re8xf8#, and the g-Pawn is pinned).

3. Re8xf8+ Kg8xf8 decoying the King to f8 where it will be hit by

4. Qg5-d8#

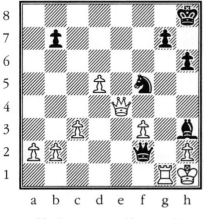

8. Black to move. Mate in four.

This attack shows a deflection, a pin and another deflection to set up another Queen checkmate.

1. ... Bh3-g2+

2. Rg1xg2 getting the Rook out of the way for a Queen check.

2. ... Qf2-f1+

3. Rg2-g1 Now the Rook is forced into a pin, while also closing in the King.

3. ... Nf5-g3+ With the Rook pinned, there is only one move:

4. h2xg3 Qf1-h3#

Mating Attacks

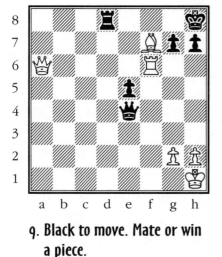

9. Black to move. Mate or win a piece.

Both Kings appear vulnerable on the back Rank. It is Black to move, and caution is urged. Taking the Rook with 1. …g7xRf6 ends badly: 2. Qa6xf6#. And 1. …Rd8-d1 is easily stopped by the convergence of the White Queen and Rook on f1: 2. Rf6-f1 blocks the attack. However, there is an interesting interception/deflection in

1. …**Qe4-c6!** If White takes the Queen with either the Rook or the Queen, mate follows on the back rank. If White doesn't take the Queen, Black wins a piece.

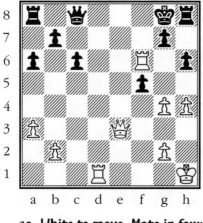

10. White to move. Mate in four.

This game ended in a pretty epaulette mate after a couple of neat deflections.

1. **Rd1-d8+** deflecting the Black Queen from her attack on e6.

1. …   **Qc8xd8**
2. **Qe3-e6+ Kg8-h7**
3. **Rf6xh6+** deflecting the Pawn from g7 and decoying it to h6.

3. …   **g7xh6** Now there is a nice open line to the Black King, and the King is also blocked in on both sides by the Rook on h8 and the Pawn on h6.

4. **Qe6-f7#**

Mating Attacks

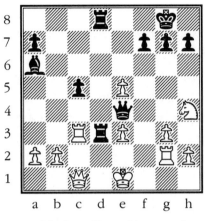

11. Black to Move. Mate in three.

Black has a well-posted Bishop on a6 slicing through the White King's position, backing up doubled Rooks on the open d-file and a centralized Queen. With such an awesome lineup, there should be a mating attack.

| 1. | ... | Qe4xe3+ |

2. **Qc1xe3** Blocking with the Rook, 2. Rg2-e2 leads to 2. ... Qe3-g1#. And it's also all over after 2. Ke1-f1, Rd3-d1++#.

| 2. | ... | Rd3-d1+ |
| 3. | Ke1-f2 | Rd1-f1# |

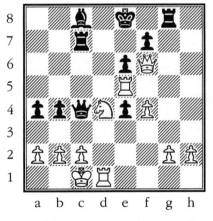

12. White to move. Mate in three.

A decoy, a double check and a mate. Three moves and White gets the point.

1. **Qf6-d8+** lures the King into a double check.

1.	...	Ke8xd8
2.	Nd4-c6++	Kd8-e8
3.	Rd1-d8#	

Mating Attacks

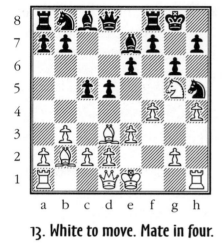

13. White to move. Mate in four.

White has a fine pair of Bishops raking the Black King's field. In addition, there is that powerful Knight sitting on g5, and a Queen on d1 with an open diagonal leading to the action around the Black King.

1. **Qd1xh5** the threat of mate in one at h7 forces Black to do something. But 1. ...g6xh5 falls to 2. Bd3xh7#, so Black tries

1. ... **Be7xg5** running into the surprise

2. **Qh5xh7+**   **Kg8xh7**
3. **h4xg5dis+**   **Kh7-g8**
4. **Rh1-h8#**

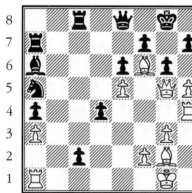

14. White to Move. Mate in four.

Here Fischer has a powerful assault on the Black King, while the majority of the Black pieces are off on the Queenside. It isn't wise to let anyone—especially Bobby Fischer—get such a strong grouping of pieces and Pawns around the King.

1. **Qg5-h6**   **Qe8-f8**
2. **Qh6xh7+!Kg8xh7**
3. **h5xg6++** Now 3. ...Kh7-g8 is mate after 4. Rh4-h8#.

3. ... **Kh7xg6** but this is no better.

4. **Bg2-e4#**

Mating Attacks

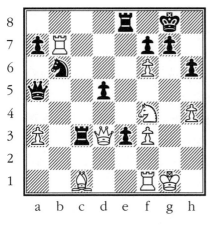

15. White to move. Mate in three.

A knowledge of the Rook and Knight patterns gave Bronstein a quick victory in this position.

1. Qd3-g6!! The threat of mate on g7 compels Black to capture the Queen.

1. ...   f7xg6
2. Rb7xg7+   Kg8-f8 (or h8)
3. Nf4xg6#
4. Nf4xg6#

16. White to move. Mate in four.

White's forces are well coordinated for the attack. A clever deflection of the Black Queen starts the damage.

1. Qd4-a4+ Qa5xa4

(1. ... Ke8-f8 loses the Queen in a hopeless situation)

2. Nd5-c7+   Ke8-f8
3. Rd1xd8+   Qa4-e8
4. Rd8xe8#

Mating Attacks

17. White to move. Mate in three.

The Black King appears to be relatively safe, surrounded by two Pawns, a Rook and Knight, and the Black Queen zeroing in from afar.

Appearances are deceptive, however, as the Black fort comes crashing down after White hits it with a surprise Queen sacrifice.

    1.   Qd3xa6+   b7xa6 the only move.

    2.   Nc7-b5++   Ka7-a8 again, the only move.

    3.   Re7-a7#

18. Black to move. Mate in three.

This position should give hope to every student who ever plays chess. It's from a scholastic game played by an 800 level fourth grader named Chris Mayfield. Chris felt he must have something here, and spent twenty minutes in deep concentration before making the first move of the following splendid combination.

    1.   ...   Bg2-e4!! blocking out the e5 Rook and threatening an immediate mate on g2.

    2.   Qc1-f1   Nf4-e2+ Deflecting the Queen. If the Rook weren't blocked out, this would not work. Now, however, there is only one move to escape check. The Queen must capture the Knight.

    3.   Qf1xe2   Qh3-g2#

The author hopes that this excursion into the wonderful world of checkmate patterns will only be the beginning of your exploration of this fascinating and essential part of the great game of chess. There are many fine books on checkmates, carrying these ideas to a much more complex level. The more you study, the better you will be at finding the winning moves. Keep reading, and you will be well rewarded for your efforts.